10/11/10

To Connie Luck

Praying you are blessed as you
read.
May God's light shine through you

Barbara Holloway

FROM COTTONFIELDS TO MISSION FIELDS

BARBARA A. HOLT HOLLOWAY

authorHOUSE®

AuthorHouse™
1663 Liberty Drive
Bloomington, IN 47403
www.authorhouse.com
Phone: 1-800-839-8640

First published by AuthorHouse   5/12/2009

ISBN: 978-1-4389-8332-5 (sc)

Printed in the United States of America
Bloomington, Indiana

This book is printed on acid-free paper.

DEDICATION

To my Lord and Savior Jesus Christ; and the Holy Spirit, who is in truth the Author. "Jesus Christ is the author and the finisher of our faith" (Hebrews 12:2) . To my wonderful, God- given husband, Christopher Holloway, for his many years of love and devotion, as well as his servant's heart. Thank you Chris for your unwavering support, encouragement and your faith in what God has done in me. My children Vincent, Chris Jr., Anthony, LaShondra, Yvette, Chrissy and Adrienne, you continually inspire me to grow beyond myself. To my seventeen grandchildren who I look forward to seeing continue the family legacy of ministry. To my boss, Dr. John Menius, who often shared with me how he thought my life's story was inspiring. He encouraged me to write a book, and said if no one else reads it, "I will. " Thank you, Dr. Menius for being a vessel which God used to get this done. My Pastor, Bishop Anita W. Kelley, Way of Life Church, St. Louis, MO. Thank you, Bishop Kelley, for the example of a life given over to God. You demonstrate God's character in fullness. Just as my father was my first Pastor that God used to steer me, you are the Pastor God has used to develop me. I am grateful to God for giving me "pastors according to mine heart, which shall feed you with knowledge and understanding." Jeremiah 3: 15. I am also grateful for the other pastors in my life, the late Elder Clarence Guydon, Pastor D.L. O'Neal, Pastor William Z. Mathews and Dr. and Mrs. Ken Van Dine who served as my spiritual mentors in the mission field of Haiti. I also want to thank my family, my siblings, my friends and extended family, the entire Holt family, the Jeffery family and the Holloway family. I am grateful to God for the blessing of having a family who loves the Lord and have determined to serve Him throughout eternity. Finally, I thank God for the many spiritual mentors, surrogate mothers, friends and the members of Way of Life Church, St. Louis Missouri, whom God has used to impart wisdom and knowledge unto me. You served as endless vessels of rich love and blessings. May God reward you for your giving and service unto His Kingdom. My prayer is that it will bring glory and honor to our Heavenly Father and inspire all who read it to give their lives to Jesus Christ.

PREFACE AND INTRODUCTION

Proverbs 13:22a. Says "A good man leaveth an inheritance for his children's children"

My father, Arthur D. Holt, was indeed a "good" man. Dad wrote his autobiography when he was seventy-one years old. As you read his story you can see the grace of God poured out over his life and the life of his children. God was able to accomplish much through him, as he lived his life as a servant of God, a Pastor and minister of the household of faith. A key element in his life was his unwavering faith in God, like Job, that took him beyond his circumstances. We witnessed in his life perseverance and determination to do the will of the Heavenly Father. My father passed away on January 9th, 2008, after battling Alzheimer's disease for five years. He was able to accomplish completing his life story before his mind began to dim. God saw fit to allow him the window to tell his story that others might know the faithfulness and love of God. Growing up in rural Arkansas in the 1930's his family faced many challenges. By the time he was twelve years old both of his parents had died and he had become the "bread winner" of the family. He and his other six siblings lived with extended family members until he joined the army at age eighteen. Dad never forgot the difficult times and challenges in his life, and he never forgot those who helped him along the way. He would tell his story often to his children so they too would know the faithfulness of the God he served. His story is an amazing journey of God's grace in the face of insurmountable odds. The Carpenter, a Family Legacy, is his story and it is weaved into my story. His story inspired me to continue sharing more about our family. I continue telling of the grace of God over our lives as we grow up in abject poverty in rural Arkansas, face racism as mandatory integration of public schools begins, work as tenant farm hands, all as we grow up in the church. As I tell this story you will see how God uses ordinary individuals in our lives. They impart love, courage, direction, wisdom, vision and unwavering faith. They serve as spiritual mentors, surrogate parents and vessels of great strength. God placed many such people in my life and this story is written to acknowledge what God was able to accomplish through servants who focused more on others than themselves. It is my prayer that this story will inspire all who read it to live their lives for the glory of God. At my father's funeral I shared some childhood memories about him and the impact he had on my life. This is what I shared that day: When I was about five or six years old I remember standing in the front yard of a house. I was looking across the field about two miles away and pointing to the home we lived in. I remember crying and saying "Daddy, I want to go home". Dad picked me up and said, "You are home," Many years later my father would share this story with the family. He had been working as a tenant farmer living in the house provided by the land owner, consequently we moved around a lot. We had lived in this particular two- story home for most of my life. It was my earliest memory of home. On the day we moved out, I could see that house from the front yard of the new home. Dad said that when I was crying and asking to go home, he knew he had to build a permanent home for his family. He said that was the motivation for him to buy property and build a permanent home for his family. Later, he would build that home and he would raise his family there. I share this story because in this I can see my earthly father, depicting the Heavenly Father who desires to pick us up when we are wandering around from place to place, He lovingly picks us up and introduces us to His Son, Jesus the Divine Carpenter, and lets us know HE has built an eternal home for us. Some years later after we had moved into the new home, I was home from school with the flu. I remember I felt nauseated, and ran to the bathroom to vomit. I hated the feeling of vomiting. I was crying and heaving. Dad came into the bathroom and cleaned me up, sat me on the counter top, and consoled me. He said, "It's gonna be ok gal, go back to bed." In this account I see the Love of God, and how He has provided a way to heal us from the sickness of sin, through HIS Son Jesus, who by his stripes we are healed.

When I was about ten years old, while getting ready for school, I could not find anything appropriate to wear. We were instructed to get our clothes ready the night before so we would not be scrabbling in the morning. I had not done this, so I was searching throughout my limited wardrobe trying to find something to wear. I was only able to fine one dress that was clean, but it was torn. It had a tear around the collar and on the chest area. Since I was already running late to get breakfast and out the door, I decided this was my only option. But to cover up the torn and tattered portion, I put my winter coat on and buttoned it up all the way, so no one could see the tear. As I left my bedroom, on my way out the door and passing through the kitchen, Dad was at the kitchen table, he called me back and said, "Let me see what you have on". As I unbuttoned my coat, and he saw the condition of my dress, he said "oh no, you can't go to school like this, we have to get you some more clothes. You just won't be able to go to school today." This account reveals to me that our Heavenly Father does care about our garments. He has given us a robe of righteousness, in Christ Jesus, so that when HE looks at us He sees the Righteousness of Christ, and not our filthy rags. Our righteousness is as filthy rags in the eyesight of God. So I am grateful for all God has given unto us, through HIS Son Jesus Christ. My father was a man of great spiritual strength. His love for God and his family were evident in the principles he was determined to pass on to his children. My life is a result of the father who sacrificed so much for his family. Growing up in a family surrounded by ministers of God, as a child I knew the name of the Lord. However, it would be many years later that I would come to know HIM intimately for myself. It was indeed my earthly father who showed me the way to the eternal Father, God. In this story I pray you see the grace of God, all who God is going out in behalf of those HE loves. In 1986 following the death of our father's sister Leatha Mae Peebles, our aunt Sista, asked me and my siblings to plan a family reunion and research the family history. In researching our family history, we noted that the Holt family had a minister or pastor in every generation. It was then that I begin to see the call of God on the life of our family as like unto Abraham. Our family had been called by God for ministry and it would define our legacy. My life is a result of the grace of God in full measure poured out upon a family. Now I know that my life is a result of God's divine plan and purpose for this family. All that I am and ever hope to be is because of Christ Jesus and HIS love unto me. In writing this story my hope and prayer is that you will see the many people God uses to bring a person unto HIMSELF. We often times lose site of the fact that we are here on earth for a divine purpose. We can get caught up in our own thinking and our own plans, but God is Sovereign. He and He alone is in control of our lives, ultimately He pursues us back to Himself. Then and then alone will our lives be meaningful and whole. We will not experience life and that more abundantly apart from God and His Son Jesus Christ our Savior and Lord. What you will read in these writings are brief memories from my childhood and young adult life, in telling these stories, please keep in mind that there was a foundation laid that kept me in the path of God. Going from the cotton fields of Arkansas to the Mission fields of Haiti and beyond is a testimony of the amazing grace of God.

BACK COVER STORY

This is an autobiographic and inspirational story of the author's life. This story details the divine hand of God and His grace through personal challenges and difficult circumstances. The author uses excerpts from her father's autobiography to give the reader two perspectives of the events. Throughout you will see how God uses ordinary individuals to guide us into His purpose. It is with much gratitude that I write this story in acknowledgement of what God has done in my life. God used many pastors, spiritual mentors, surrogate parents and vessels of love to dispense His amazing grace unto me. My life's journey from the cotton fields to the mission field of Haiti is a testimony to this grace.

COTTON FIELDS TO MISSION FIELDS

Barbara A. Holt Holloway

Daddy said one year after he and mother had married she became quite ill. Apparently she had symptoms from joint and muscle pain to fatigue and skin rashes. Along with those symptoms she exhibited intolerance to heat and could not work in the fields. During the cotton picking season everyone in the family needed to work to increase the income. Mother usually worked as the accountant for the cotton season, keeping the records of amounts of cotton picked per field hand and dispensing the monetary compensation at the end of the work day. Dad tells us that he didn't know what to do, so he began taking her to area doctors, and eventually when there seemed no hope the local doctor recommended her care to the university doctors in Little Rock, Arkansas. The university specialists were unable to determine the cause of her illness. Desiring to find some relief for her pain and discomfort, dad resorted to taking mom to the baths in Hot Springs, Arkansas. The warm waters of the natural springs helped soothe and ease her joint pain. During this time the family continued to grow. Whenever mom would have a baby she would go to her mother's home and the local midwife would deliver the child. I was the first of her children to be born in a doctor's office or clinic. Dr. Pupsta, a local general practitioner in Clarendon on the White River was the only physician that delivered babies at his clinic. Most people were still relying on midwives. This was 1956 when many people still did not have indoor plumbing, including our family. I have to wonder if mother's health condition was the reason Dad decided to go to a clinic. God is faithful unto His people and HE is forever working things out for our good and for His purpose. When I was born I was not surrounded by the immediate family as in a home delivery by midwives. My entrance into this world was different and today I see that God had something different in store for me. The world changes for our immediate family when each of us is born. Our entrance into this life changes the dynamics in our families, our homes as well as our extended family. God uses us to bring change, most of the time we do not notice it in the physical realm but there is indeed a spiritual change when we come into existence. Our family dynamics and relationships change to further extend the love of God to another person.

Daddy's words: "A year or so after the wife and I got married, she began to have skin problems. Small water blisters would appear on her face and arms. When they would burst, they would leave a raw spot that didn't seem to heal properly and they kept getting worse. She started visiting the doctor regularly, but he didn't seem to help at all. About the same time as my wife's problem, my sister Earnestine (who we nicknamed Totsie) begin having nose bleeds. Many times she would bleed so much she would pass out. I would have to pick her up as you would a baby and literally carry her into the doctor's office. She and my wife were visiting the same doctor in Stuttgart, Arkansas. His name was Dr. J.B. Bryant, the only black doctor in the area. My wife was visiting Dr. Bryant very often until 1951. We then got an appointment to go to the University Hospital in Little Rock, Arkansas. She was treated at this hospital for about a year or so. Earnestine was also sent to the hospital to be treated for her nose bleeds. She would sometimes have to go twice a week. Then finally, in 1952, the doctors gave Earnestine an operation which stopped the nose bleed. They said she had a tumor in the upper nose. But they could not help my wife's skin problem. Sometime later, my wife was referred to a clinic in Hot Springs, Arkansas. She stayed there one month or six weeks. Yet no cure. Finally, my wife started going to a doctor in Clarendon, Arkansas. She continued with this doctor for some ten or twelve years and still no cure. The skin problem didn't seem to interfere with anything else. We still had children and they were all healthy with no visible problems. My wife was not able to work out in the cotton fields when it was hot because of the skin problem. She started making plans to teach school, but needed a few hours of class work. The skin problem got progressively worse, so that ideal was stopped. So she became the best housewife she could be and helped in the things she could do."

My early childhood years were spent surrounded by my siblings and my grandparents. Since mother was sick a lot, we spent a lot of time at grandma's house. Whenever mom would have another baby we would spend a week or two at grandmas, while mom was recuperating. Our home was actually about ten miles from our maternal grandmother's house. We lived on sharecropper property in the rural area of Arkansas County. The house consisted of four rooms -two bedrooms with a small living area and kitchen. There was no indoor plumbing and our heat was from a pot- bellied wood stove that was the center piece in the living room. The outdoor toilet was located behind the house about two hundred yards surrounded by brush and trees. There usually was a Sears Roebuck catalog or Walter Field catalog in the outhouse for use as toilet paper. Water was used sparingly, and typically a hot bath was reserved for Saturday nights in a # 2 galvanized wash tub. The rest of the time your daily hygiene was a thorough hand washing with plenty of soap. Mother spent most of her days lying on the sofa in the living room with a television tray at her side filled with medications. Although she was weak and didn't have the strength to do many things with us, she loved to read with us. She would ask my older sister, Ruthie, to check out books from the school library for her. I can still remember her voice, soft and reassuring, even as she laid suffering in pain. Since Ruthie was the oldest child at home, a great deal of the day to day household tasks would fall upon her. Mother would discipline us from her sick bed on the sofa. I remember my sister Diane, who must have been about eight or nine years old at the time decided to play horseback with our younger brother Theodore, who was about five. She sat on his back and he collapsed on the floor in pain. Mother immediately told my sister Ruthie to go and get a belt. Mother was going to dispense some punishment to Diane. I remember thinking at the time, how could she do this from the sofa, but she did. Diane never again used any other siblings as riding instruments. Mother had to have experienced pain and loss of energy to do this, but I believe she did not want to let us think because she was ill we could get away without being disciplined. Of course there was further punishment when Dad got home. Our house was in poor condition and most winters Dad had to cover the windows with plastic sheeting to keep the bitter wind out. My brother Theodore and I slept in a bunk bed in our parents' bedroom.   The other four children slept in the larger bedroom on cots and make -shift beds.   One night while lying in bed I happened to wake up and see my mother getting ready for bed.   As she was preparing for bed, she took off her wig.   That was the first time I realized mother didn't have any hair.   I didn't know what to think.   Why didn't my mother have hair?   Something in that moment let me know my mother was not well.   The following day I was up and asking questions.   My mom let me comb her hair to assure me she was ok.   I realize now that she wore a wig because all her hair had fallen out due to the illness.   I stood on a stool and mom sat in the chair while I brushed her hair.   While brushing her hair she sang a spiritual song and tried to teach me the words.   You know God knows what a person needs to give them assurance and security.   Standing there brushing my mom's hair gave me a sense of safety and security.   Her hair was real to me.   Looking back on this incident today, I see God preparing me for the loss of my mother.   What is even most profound to me is seeing the grace of God over our lives.   On May 13, 1963, the day after Mother's Day, our mother passed away at the age of thirty-five.   She left behind my father and seven children.   My oldest brother, Cleo, was fifteen at the time and lived with our grandmother.   At home with dad, was my older sister Ruthie, age 14, Wilma Diane, age nine, Winnie, age eight, and myself, age six, my brother Theodore ,age five ,and our youngest sister, Jackie age two.   Our lives would forever change following mother's death.   I remember the morning she died very vividly.   Dad had gotten up early that morning to go across the creek to bring Mom's mother.   He must have known and sensed during the night a significant change in mother's condition.   When I woke up that morning, grandmother, and my father's sister, Aunt Rosie, we all called her "Sista ",, and my father's surrogate mother, Girstine Jeffery were all in the back bedroom behind the kitchen.   Dad gathered us all on the living room couch and began to tell us our mother had passed away.   I looked through the curtain over the kitchen entrance and saw my grandmother with her hands over her face.   She appeared to be laughing because her shoulders were moving up and down forcefully.   But upon closer inspection, I could see tears coming down her face.   I knew something was really wrong. Aunt Sista and "Dew baby" as Mother Jeffery was affectionately called, were crying as well. Somehow I realized this was a sad day. In my mind at age six, I did not understand the concept of death or "passing "away, so even as dad shared the news with us, I could not sense the real meaning. Dad began to gather us one by one to go see our mother. She was lying in the back bedroom covered and when I entered the room, my aunt and grandmother were turning her over. Underneath her bed linens were layers of newspaper. I thought this was puzzling. Years later as a nurse, I understood that the layers of newspaper were there to protect the bed linen from soiling secondary to body waste. As I looked upon my mother's face, she appeared to be sleeping to me. What did this all really mean? My mother is "passing away" or has "passed away. After each of us had seen mother, Dad announced that a man named "Booker" would be coming to get her. Shortly thereafter a long black car pulled into our front drive area and backed up to the back bedroom door. I started crying along with my other siblings, I did not want the "Booker" man to take my mother anywhere. Our grandmothers and aunt consoled us and tried to explain what was happening as they moaned and wailed with us. My father assisted the "Booker "man in taking mother out on a long stretcher. I learned many years later that the "Booker" man was the local undertaker; his name was Booker Releford, the owner of the only black funeral home in Stuttgart. That same morning I remember the school bus pulling up to our house and dad sending my sister Diane out to inform the bus driver that we would not be going to school that week because our mother had just died. That week was a whirlwind week in my mind. I remember that a lot of my mother's relatives started arriving from up north, primarily Chicago. Mother had two brothers and one sister living in Chicago and they all begin arriving with their families. My mother's funeral was scheduled for the following Sunday. I remember being excited about riding in my uncle's new car. While we were driving, my uncle asked me if I wanted to go live with him in Chicago. He was one of my favorite uncles, because when he came to visit us he would always pick me up and toss me in the air. He would also tease and joke with us a lot, he was really funny. He was a very tall man, about six eleven or more, so when he picked you up you felt as though you could touch the clouds. Getting to ride in his car was a treat for me and I was looking forward to having a fun day with him. When we arrived at the funeral home my uncle pulled in behind a line of cars and I asked him what we were doing. He said, don't you know your mother died and we are going to her funeral? This information did not mean anything to me because I could not grasp the meaning of death. I remember that morning getting ready for the funeral, several aunts and family members were at our house helping get the children ready. I had a beautiful taffeta white dress I had worn as a flower girl in one of my mother's cousin's wedding. I loved that dress. It was white, full and fluffy. The dress had a taffeta petticoat underneath that made the dress stand and flair outward. I also had a brand new pair of black patent leather shoes. There was great care given unto us to dress us that day. Each child was dressed in beautiful new clothes and shoes. It seemed a festive occasion to my mind. Arriving at the church I remember seeing all the cars and people outside. The church was a wood frame -one room building with wooden pews. After getting settled in the church we all sat on the front row. There were a lot of people in the church, actually standing room only, not a difficult thing considering the size of the building.   Sitting on the front pew with us was Ms. Mae Jane Clemmons. She was the local midwife and also an usher/nurse for the church. Ms Mae Jane had in fact delivered most of my mother's babies, so she knew our family quite intimately.   She kept fanning us with a paper fan. Between her tears and wailing she would mutter, "poor motherless children".   I kept wondering what she meant by "motherless children."   As I looked around the church, I saw many faces of people I knew as well as people I did not know. I was anxiously looking and waiting for my best friend Vera to come into the church. As the mourners began filing past my mother's coffin, many were crying and sobbing. Several women had to be assisted from the church. I was peeking around every adult in line frantically looking for my best friend. Suddenly, I saw her mother, father, and one of her sisters in the line. Boy, did that make me happy- but still no Vera. I knew in my heart she would be there;

after all we were best friends. I just knew Vera would be right behind them. After the family had filed past the coffin, my disappointment rose, as I realized she was not with them. I started crying, I wonder if Ms. May Jane thought I was crying about my mother because she started consoling me by patting me on the back. I was crying because my best friend did not come to my mother's funeral. As I have said, I did not have a concept of death, so I wasn't sad about my mother. Finally, the funeral director moved the coffin close to our row. Ms. Mae Jane said, "Stand up babies and look at your mother." Mother was lying there in the coffin dressed in a pink chiffon gown, clasping a white bible wearing white gloves. The image of my mother in her coffin is still very vivid to me today. I was six years old at the time and it has left a lifelong impression upon me. My older sister, Ruthie, starting crying which set off the rest of us. Eventually, as we took our seats again, the baby, Jackie, was so restless and fretful, that Ms. Mae Jane asked Ruthie to take her out of the church. There are few other details about the funeral that I remember, but others shared their memories with me in later years. The one thing that stood out most for me is that my friend Vera did not come. The following Monday as we returned to school, many of the children had attended our mother's funeral with their parents and were asking me questions. I felt quite special going into school the next morning amidst all the attention. I remember telling another friend, almost boastfully, "My mother died and they had her funeral yesterday." These words were spoken out of the mouth of a child who had no concept of the finality of death and the great expanse of grief that accompanies that knowledge. Later that day at school I asked Vera why she did not come to my mother's funeral. Vera told me she was fully dressed that morning but couldn't find her Sunday shoes. She looked all over the house frantically searching for them. Finally her mother and sister started helping her look for them. She started crying and crying. Vera's mother said it would be okay if she didn't go. Vera stressed that she must go because I was her best friend. After searching all over the house they could not find the shoes. Her mother sadly informed Vera that she could not go and they had to leave or they would be late. She cried after they left for most of the day.   When they returned they gave her an account of the funeral. They told Vera they saw me looking for her. When they sat down for dinner that evening in the dining room Vera pulled out her chair from the table and sat down. Low and behold she sat on her Sunday shoes.   They were on the dining room chair.

In Daddy's Words: "My wife was still getting worse with the skin problem. I was still making plans to build us a home on the deeded plot. One thing I had in mind was that I never wanted to move my children any more. I wanted them to have a home site. Many of the rural people were getting new homes built through the Shell Home Program from Jim Walters and many other companies. I was hoping and praying to build my own. By 1962, my work had grown tremendously. I had begun to install cabinets for Sears Roebuck through contracts and I also did some remodeling for them. Learning this cabinet skill early in my carpentry career sure was beneficial. It took off like wild fire. One thing I want you to know is that up until 1955, the Lord got my attention and turned my life around. Since then he has been my guide and leader. He has guided my career up to now with his blessings and I do thank Him. In 1962, my wife's skin problem had taken its toll. She lost a lot of weight and got very weak. She continued to visit the doctor every week or so, but saw no improvements. She was getting worse. As I mentioned in the beginning, I thank God for what my mother had taught me as a child. These were the times that all she had taught me would be needed and useful. My children were small and in school. Many mornings, my wife did not feel like getting up. She was getting weaker. So I would have to get the children up, prepare breakfast and get them off to school. Then I would have to go to work myself. Early training from my mother had truly prepared me for this task. In May 1963, my wife passed away. She left seven lovely children and I vowed to raise them all together, except the one that had lived with his grandmother from a baby. I conferred with the doctor about her skin problem and he told me that she had what was known at that time as a skin cancer which had turned inward in the last stages. I had many people that wanted me to give them either one or two of my children and my answer was no because I was going to keep my own children.

We found out sometime later that many of my mother's siblings wanted to take one or two of us to live with them. But Dad was adamant about us all staying together, and told them if they could not take all of us that they would not take one. He wanted us to all stay together. So the decision was made that he would keep us all with him. This indeed was a daunting task now and especially in 1963. A single man with seven children to provide for and nurture; how would he be able to do this? Only God knew. When my father was twelve years old both of his parents died two months apart. His father died in early March of 1938 from tuberculosis; and his mother in May from complications during childbirth. The seven Holt children would go to live with extended family members. Dad would assume the role of parent for his younger siblings. The amazing grace that had sustained him during this time would be sufficient for what he was facing now. There were several women in our family that served as surrogate mothers to us throughout the years. Dad's sisters, Dew Baby Jeffery, many other aunts and cousins as well as women in the neighborhood that knew our mother and felt a need to see after us. We would find out some thirty years later as my older sister Ruthie was diagnosed with lupus that our mother had the same disease. Ruthie said she remembered mother having the same "butterfly" rash across her face and similar symptoms she experienced. In 1963 there was very little known then about collagen tissue disorders, like lupus, fibromyalgia, sarcoidosis and scleroderma. I would be diagnosed with sarcoidosis at age thirty-eight. Another aunt would be diagnosed with scleroderma and a sister with arthritis. The collagen tissue disorders were plaguing our family.

Some time passed and we began adjusting to mother's death. Our father hired his sister Earnestine, "Totsie" to stay with us. She was single and it was more convenient for her to stay than for us to go somewhere while dad worked. Totsie cooked and cleaned for us. She also taught us about feminine grooming. I remember her showing us how to use underarm deodorant. The brand name of the deodorant was "Mum." It was creamy and white; what a mess we made the first couple of times we used Mum. That first year of mother's death is not that memorable to me. I remember that we spent a lot of time with other relatives, aunts and cousins. God's grace was evident over our lives in that we were five young girls exposed to other relatives and none of us were ever molested. We found out in later years that we had an uncle who molested other family members. God was watching over the "little motherless children." The following year our dad remarried a much younger woman. She was in her twenties. She had no idea what she was getting into by marrying a man with seven children. The first few months were quite challenging for all of us. She could not cook and we made it our business to remind her of that fact repeatedly. Nancy, our stepmother, was from St. Louis, MO. She had been visiting her aunt in Arkansas when she met our father. Keep in mind that he was of course very much aware that he needed a wife and mother for his children. Life changed somewhat for us as we had to adjust to having someone else take on the role of our mother. We had been operating as the housekeeper, cook, and caregiver to one another. We now had to let his wife take her place as the homemaker, wife and mother. After our father married, Totsie went back to town to live with another brother. Dad's sister, affectionately called "Sista" began doing more things for us on a regular basis. Her given name was Rosie Lee and she and her husband had eleven children of their own. Sista served as a spiritual mentor and a surrogate mother. Listening to her sing songs of praise to God and seeing her steadfastness in serving Him was inspirational. We would attend church with her quite often. One of the most impacting aspects of Sista's character was her ability to love. Somehow, miraculously, she could extend her household food beyond feeding twelve to feeding an additional seven or eight. Something near to five loaves and three fishes to feed multitudes. This was a family who lived on less than the average poverty level at that time, but somehow always managed to have more than enough. Whenever we would show up at her house she would be all smiles. In spite of her daily responsibilities of caring for her family she always had time to dispense love and care to all of us. We cherished spending time in her presence. She had joy that surpassed our understanding at the time. She would remain unmoved by her bleak and sometimes dire financial circumstances.

She trusted God and let us know quite often that was where her hope could be found. Sista was truly used by God as an example of His love for me. At a time when I had lost my mother, she became a comforter, counselor and protector. She was given the additional assignment of "pressing "our hair. Dad had five girls and he did not have a clue about the care of our hair. Now to further explain, we did not have "good" hair. We washed our hair with well water. There was no such thing as conditioner and we used grease to press our hair. Needless to say, we had hard, coarse hair that required straightening. Sista would regularly wash and press our hair usually on weekends. She became an influence for our spiritual care as well. Both of my father's sisters who lived locally belonged to the Church of God in Christ. They were strong women of God filled with the Holy Ghost. We would accompany Sista to church whenever she had an opportunity to go. From a very early age I remember our father being very concerned about us having a foundation in the church. Dad had belonged to the Church of God in Christ for many years but after he could not reconcile a concern he had with the church regarding the scriptures, he left and became a Seventh Day Adventist. However, he still allowed us to go and fellowship at the local Church of God in Christ with his sisters. We practiced the doctrines of both faiths. On Saturday's we were not allowed to do any manual work as Dad observed his Sabbath. Our dietary habits followed the Levitical code so there was no pork allowed in the house. Dad would gather us all in the living room and have church school every Saturday morning. We would read from the Bible and he would sing songs of praise to God as he strummed on his guitar. He usually tried to teach us a song our two as well. Dad had taught himself to play the guitar and would regularly play at local churches accompanying some of the gospel singers. Whenever he was practicing his guitar you could be sure he would gather us around to hear him play and sing. Dad would conduct church services every Saturday morning in our living room. The service usually lasted about an hour, and we would be very anxious to get off the couch and go watch cartoons. On Sunday's we would go to church with Sista and stay most of the day. Back then, church started around eleven in the morning and usually about three or four in the afternoon we would be heading home. At church there would be much singing and praising, shouting and speaking in tongues. This type of worship was not foreign to us in that our entire family had been a part of the Church for many years. We received our foundations in the scriptures there. Every Christmas, Easter and other special occasions the children and young adults were expected to recite scriptures and poems. I was always very reluctant to participate, because I was so shy. The older women of the church did not take no for an answer, so there was no getting out of it. They considered that paramount to saying "no" to God. I would stand in front of the church reciting what had been assigned to me with much fear and anxiety. It would be years later that I finally would get past this fear, as God developed me to speak before a congregation. Sista was very gifted in singing and usually would be on program to sing a solo or two. She was a short and stout woman, around five feet tall weighing about two hundred and thirty pounds. Even at that size she was very agile on her feet and could shout and dance for the Lord with ease. Sista and her husband were very poor and often did not have their own transportation; consequently Sista would have to wait for others to take her to church. Because of a lack of personal transportation she only made it to the church service once per month. We lived in the country with dirt roads. So in the winter time with rains and snow made the roads nearly impassable. Our church going was more frequent in the spring and summer as opposed to the winter months. However, even though Sista missed going to church, she spent her days at home praying and praising God. Her life was an example of someone, who despite their lot in life, was determined to praise and glorify God. She was a saint that praised God in advance, when things were good, and when things were not good. She always had praise for God and this joy she had made her a magnet for her nieces and nephews. She didn't seem to mind having all the extra mouths around to feed. What a great vessel of love! Her capacity to love was tremendous. Her love of God was tangible and arresting. God used her in such a way to prepare me for life that I have difficulty even expressing it. We spent a lot of time at Sista's. She was the one we turned to as teenagers when we needed advice about love matters.   Over the years, Sista experienced many heartaches and heart breaks, but through it all she yet praised God.

In Daddy's Words: "*Before my father got real sick, he would take me to church about one mile away from our home.   The church was called Paradise Church. Boy, I really enjoyed going there. Many people would be there.   They would have a time.   There was a woman who lived just north of where we lived on another farm, named Ms. Rose Rainey.   That woman could sing!. On many church days, there were men selling goodies on the church ground, candy bars, homemade ice cream for five cents a cone, boy was it good. The candy bars, like babyruths and paydays were one cent each.   The men would be selling these goodies from their cars.   Many of them owned 1929 or 1930 T-model Fords, Chevrolets and Dodges. However, the majority of people would come to church on wagons, horseback or they simply walked. I can't remember anytime my mother went to this church.   She did not understand the teachings of the Baptist faith and would not go.   She was a member of the Holiness church up home, and there was a dividing line for her.   The most and best teaching I got from the Bible was from her.   The most joyous testimonies I heard was from what the Lord had done in many people's lives and her life.   I wanted to join the church at Grady at an early age, but she told me that I need to wait until I was old enough to know what I was doing.   She was right.*"

Getting back to my stepmother Nancy, I remember the first time I actually celebrated my birthday was after Dad married Nancy.   Her birthday was in September like mine and she said we are going to have a birthday cake and have a party.   Well, sure enough we did. I had never had a real birthday party so this has been imprinted in my memory.   There were a lot of things that Nancy brought to our family that were missing; the birthday party is just one example. She offered a balance to our home.   Our dad was a no nonsense, no frills type of person.   He just believed in the basics -nothing extra.   Nancy would add things that were fun to our house.   Over the years as she and Dad began having other children, it became harder for her to spread herself among the older children. It seemed that some insecurity began to creep into her spirit.   She always seemed to feel inadequate as our motherand it that she had a need to compete with all the other surrogate mothers for our attention. In later years these insecurities would become serious issues within their marriage.

George and Dewbaby

Less than one half mile down the gravel road from our house lived Dad's first cousin George Jeffery and his wife Girstine. We all called her "Dewbaby". This couple was of great influence in my father's life and consequently ours. My father was twelve years old when his parents died. He and his siblings came to live to live with extended family. Later George and Dewbaby would have to assume the care of these orphaned children. My father never forgot their great sacrifice and reminded us often of their place in our lives. Therefore, Dew Baby and George were seen as our "surrogate grandparents." They would remain a vital source of strength, encouragement and guidance for all of us.

In Daddy's own words: "In 1937, my father had gotten sicker. Most of the plowing was done by me. My father could not do much of anything. He would lay around most of the time. He had lost a lot of weight. The doctor was not helping at all. Somehow, with ht help of neighbors, we made the crops in 1937. Mother and I got the cotton gathered that fall. My father managed to get it to the cotton gin and to do the fall settlements. As usual, Mother and I would pick cotton for other farmers by the hundred pounds to help out and that fall was no exception. Somehow with God's help, we made it through the winter. Around February, the farmers would start getting the grounds ready for planting cotton in the spring. In 1938, my father was not able to work at all. All the plowing was done by me. There were friends next door that helped. He and I worked through and through by March, we had our ground ready. News traveled up home that my father was very sick. Around mid–March, my father's brother, Jonas came down to see him. He pleaded with my father to let him take him back home to get a good doctor's treatment. My father gave in and went with him; however, my mother did not go. About a week later, we got the news that my father had passed away. My mother was in the "family way", as being pregnant was called. She was about seven months. Two of my mother's brothers came to Grady to carry us up home to bury my father. My mother had only one sister, Aunt Maud Jeffery. Both of my grandmothers were dead, so naturally sisters would rely on each other. We had my father's funeral at Mount Pisgah Church about three fourths of a mile from where my Aunt Maud lived. Mother planned to stay with Aunt Maud for awhile, at least until she had the baby. A week or so went by and my mother got her brothers to go back to Grady to move her household goods up home. She was planning to get her a house as soon as the child was born. Shortly after we came up home, the farmers begin to get their farm land ready for the spring crops. My Aunt Maud's husband, Ed and their son George were also farmers. George was about seventeen years old and he was my role model. My mother told them how I had plowed the farmland in Grady and insisted that I could help them as well. I caught on quickly to their way of plowing we got the cotton planted and George taught me many other things, like hunting. When I came up here, I knew about plowing and fishing but nothing at all about hunting. I had never been hunting before, so George begin taking me squirrel and rabbit hunting. O course, I had no gun, but George would always loan me one of his. He taught me about hunting for different game, including deer, duck, geese and rabbits. On May 17, 1938 my mother gave birth to twin girls, sadly one of the girls was still born. Shortly after giving birth my mother begin hemorrhaging, there was no doctor available, only a mid-wife. My mother passed away that same day, leaving seven children. Now here we were having lost both parents within a two month period. But you know that God knows what he is doing and he doesn't make any mistakes. Aunt Maud and her husband managed to keep us all together and somehow they kept enough food on the table for all of us. Aunt Maud did her best for us. There was not much help that a family could get at that time from the welfare program. Aunt Maud got a little help from welfare and the Red Cross. In 1940 Aunt Maud came down with pneumonia and passed away. George had recently married Dew Baby and they had a one year old daughter. Now George and Dew Baby had to become the parents of all of us as well. We could have been sent to a foster home and put up for adoption or given to different family members, but George and Dew Baby made a tremendous sacrifice and decided we would continue to stay with them. We were never separated from them, not until we were grown-ups. Even as I write these words down, tears of joy come to my eyes as I truly thank God for them. No one could make me believe that God was not in this picture"

This couple would continue to spend their lifetime serving others and giving of themselves. God used them in great ways in our lives. They were a constant source of strength, encouragement and support to our family during very painful times. Dewbaby was a village mother, not only did she have fourteen children of her own and then take care of the seven orphaned Holt children; she extended herself in the church as a mother as well. The family would have a garden each year and it was the source of most of their food. Dewbaby could cook quite well and whenever you would visit their home there would always be plenty of beans and greens to eat. She had the ability to create a bountiful meal seemingly out of nothing. God used her to dispense love, wisdom and a dose or two of correction into our lives. She gave so much of herself to her family and many others. Only God can give a person the capacity to love beyond your own family and extend your circle of influence to a community or village. It is not humanly possible to love to that extent but by the grace God. Growing up in the church Mother Jeffery would be an example to us of unselfish love. I experienced firsthand the loving care of people such as George and Dewbaby who assisted dad with our care following mother's death. She would watch over us as a mother hen from afar, making sure we were in church and continually praying to God on our behalf. Thank God for surrogate parents, unselfishly giving of themselves to others so that orphaned children would know the love and the security that can only be found in God. It makes an eternal difference, it made a difference in our father's life and it made a difference in mine. God provided many vessels that were dispensaries of His great grace and love. George and Dewbaby Jeffery were truly two of them. Today, George and Dew baby's daughters have a restaurant in Stuttgart called "Dew Baby's" where they continue to dispense the love, wisdom, grace and compassion that their parents demonstrated as they fed many in the community. They are feeding their patrons not only physical food but spiritual nourishment as well.

DEBUT INTO THE COTTON FIELDS

I was probably about six or seven years of age when I made my debut into the cotton fields. Dad had strict rules that governed your work day. First, you pulled your own weight, in other words, as you picked cotton you were expected to pull your cotton sack along behind you, no excuses and no whining. A typical day in the cotton fields went as follows. The appropriate attire was essential to prevent sun damage; we were all instructed to wear long sleeve shirts and a wide brim hat. Many of the cotton pickers also wrapped a bath towel around their necks to absorb sweat and to protect the neckline. About five or six o'clock in the morning you were picked up by a local "hauler." The hauler was someone that the landowners hired to secure the necessary labor to get the crop harvested. This "hauler" was usually paid a flat fee per head count. After being picked up by the hauler, we were driven over to the field where we would be working for the day. The crew leader made the assignments, someone was designated as the water carrier, and someone was given the assignment of weighing all cotton sacks. However, these two individuals still picked cotton as well. There seemed to be an unofficial competitiveness within the group. Often you would hear veterans bragging about the highest weight of cotton picked in one day. Each cotton picking season someone would be crowned as the one who could "pick the most cotton in one day." Many of the seasoned veterans would quote figures of picking three hundred or more pounds of cotton per day. One of the incentives for picking large pounds was you were paid according to your weight. That was your day's wages, so the more you picked the more money you made. There were many entire families out picking cotton; father, mother, and all the children. There were often children as young as four or five years old walking alongside a parent with a small "croaker" sack. Actually, this was a community of people consisting of neighbors, family and church members. When I made my entrance into the fields, Dad put me alongside his sister Totsie. She could really pick cotton and was quite skilled at gleaning every fiber of cotton from the bolls. Because we picked very early in the morning the dew was still upon the cotton bolls. This made picking a little more difficult, but Totsie began to show me how to pull the fullness of the boll first and then glean the remainder fibers one at a time. As I pulled on the cotton fiber, the boll scratched my hands and I yelled. She just said "gal, you better get tougher than that or you will not pick any weight to amount to anything, and I know your dad won't be happy about that." So, I began pulling cotton out the boll, squeamish each time my hands touched the bolls. It was not long before I noticed I had whelps and scratches all over my hands. Finally Totsie gave me a pair of socks to put over my hands to protect them. After that I was able to move a little faster. As the morning progressed she continued to share tips for picking efficiently and effectively. It wasn't long before I encountered a worm or two on the bolls. That stopped me dead in my tracks. When I started crying and screaming she came over to me and said, "Gal, you got to be tougher than that, those worms won't bother you." "Once we made it to the end of the row, I told her my back was starting to hurt from bending over to pick the cotton. She was carrying her sack and picking two rows at a time. Her sack was over half full at this point, but she let me put my sack on her bag and she carried them both. She began to tell me that as my back muscles were strengthened. I would be able to carry more weight. Once her sack was full we went to weigh in the first morning's pickings. Many people were already in line to get weighed in. You could hear the cheers and words of competitiveness being voiced. This served as an incentive for picking more cotton. If you did not pick a certain amount you were viewed as lazy. Several people were weighing in at over fifty pounds, some eighty or ninety. Usually, the men could pick and carry nearly one hundred pounds of cotton in a full sack. So, when my little sack was weighed, I think it weighed in at about fifteen pounds. Everyone was looking at me as though they were thinking, "she is going to starve if she doesn't pick more cotton than that amount." Around noon time we would hear a bell signaling that it was time to take a lunch break. Everyone had packed a sack lunch and water was provided by the "hauler" in a huge canteen. We used the same cup to drink from but there were a few who had brought along their own drinking cup. Lunch lasted about thirty minutes. I was really tired, hot and my muscles were aching. But, I was determined to be able to pick my weight in cotton before long. After lunch I went out with renewed determination to pick more than fifteen pounds. During the second weigh in I measured about twenty pounds. I was on my way. The cotton field was a place of learning many life lessons. The adults would have serious conversations about the things going on in the world around us. There was talk about economic hardships and the way to get out of the cycle of poverty. Many of our family members had migrated to the north to work in the factories to earn better wages to care for their families. Several expressed a desire to one day escape the toiling labor in the sun that seemed to be the only means for survival in the south. Going north was always looked upon in a spiritual way, in a metaphoric way as going to the "Promised Land." Many of our relatives would return in the summer months driving new vehicles and telling stories of the "good" life up north. Many of the conversations in the cotton fields related to spiritual principles. My relatives would often quote bible verses as they worked in the sun. It was said more than once by many that "The Lord will make a way somehow." "The Lord knows everything." "Even the very numbers of hairs that are on your head are numbered." And "it's gonna be better by and by, along with "weeping may endure for a night but joy comes in the morning." Hearing them make these scriptural declarations over and over, I could only wonder if God knew how much my back ached from picking cotton and when would things get better. Listening to their stories and seeing their perseverance was an encouragement to me. They also were very vocal about the fragility of this life and would state many times their concern for your eternal life. Some of the songs they sang referred to living eternally with God. I listened in sheer wonder and at times trembled in fear as they sang about "Moving on up a little higher" "His eye is on the sparrow and I know He watches me." There were many days when the entire field of workers would launch into singing a spiritual song. I learned a lot of the songs I know today from singing in the cotton fields. It lifted your spirit and it was a way to move with music, and rhythmically pick cotton. Oftentimes we would essentially have our church choir rehearsal in the fields. The cotton fields had various lengths of rows, some were long rows and then there were some short rows. You learned early that the long rows were hard and you looked forward to getting to the short rows. At times a partner or friend would pick alongside you picking two rows at the same time. This required much skill and strength, because you were picking a row of cotton with each hand. This technique was the way most of the cotton pickers were able to pick two or three hundred pounds per day. I would never develop enough skill to pick this way, but eventually did reach a personal goal of one hundred fifty pounds picked in one day. Our life is very similar to the rows in a cotton field. We have some long rows, where the end seems so far away , but as we toil and struggle with a particular situation, thanks be to God he puts people in your life that help you on those long rows. They encourage and support you and sometimes maybe even help you pick some of the cotton off your row, so that you make it to the end together. After toiling on a long row, the short rows seem easy. Such as life, the long-lived struggles in our lives help us appreciate a short row issue. The support and encouragement I received picking cotton on those long rows was preparing me for my life of long rows. Picking cotton with my family members and other relatives served as an opportunity to hear some great stories and hear beautiful spiritual songs. There were many mornings in the cotton fields where the entire group of cotton pickers would launch out into singing. The women usually sang songs of praise to God and continually gave Him thanks for their blessings. Little did I know that this precious time in the cotton fields would be a foundation for me with spiritual mentors. Those biblical principles would serve as a guiding lamp and light for my life, as well as a source of strength in later years. Those hot summer days in the cotton fields were more than just a way to earn income for a family, but a gathering of souls to bring in a harvest. Many of us were prepared for a life of laboring in the fields for the Kingdom of God.

In Daddy's Words:

"By the time I was five and a half, my mother begin to take me to the cotton fields to help chop and pick cotton. When the home crops were done, mother and father would pick and chop cotton by hire. Chopping by the day was $.70 cent and picking was $.35 cent per hundred pounds. On the Ray Wood farm, most of the women would work in the fields from early morning until eleven o'clock. They would go home to prepare the noon meal and then come back in the afternoon. After working in the fields all day, they would then go home to prepare supper. I know my mother would be very tired after supper was finished. She would instruct my sister, Rosie and me to wash the dishes. If I failed to do them, she would get my bottom just as much as my sister Rosie. At the time I thought she was too hard on me about washing dishes, but as the years went by and I had my own family, I would thank God for what my mother had taught me."

In the cotton fields I found it hard to understand how they could sing and be happy while under such physical labor and hardship. It was many years later after I had come to an intimate relationship with the Lord Jesus Christ that I received revelation of why they could sing this spiritual song. "I sing because I'm happy, I sing because I 'm free, His eye is on the sparrow, and I know He watches me. " That is an old Negro spiritual song that has been sung over generations as the Negroes worked on the plantation fields and suffered great persecution. This and other Negro spirituals served as a song of praise and victory over their present suffering. Knowing that this present suffering is no comparison to what we will experience in glory as we live eternally with Christ. The Apostle Paul said, "For our light affliction, which is but for a moment, is working for us a far more exceeding and eternal weight of glory" (2 Corinthians 4: 17). My aunts and other relatives could sing this song as a personal testimony because they had come to understand that they were free and that they had victory in Christ Jesus. During my years of working in the cotton fields I learned many spiritual lessons. These principles would sustain me in my personal life later. God had a plan for my life and it would be through all these life experiences that He would shape my character and mold me into a vessel He could use. It is God's desire that we all come to a place in Him, whereby our lives are no longer ours but HIS to use for His glory.

In 1964 we moved from a sharecropper's home to a home on property our father had purchased. Dad had spent many evenings down the road at this house trying to complete it. He did not have access to large sums of money, so the work had to be done as he had funds for supplies. During the early fall of that year, our butane tank was running low. Dad did not have additional money to refill the tank, but he did have a full tank at the new home place. He made the decision to move us on down the road to the house he was building as our permanent home. The new house was not completed. The only rooms with walls and insulation were the kitchen, bathroom and two bedrooms. The living room and the two additional bedrooms were not finished. I remember looking around at the open walls and seeing the ceiling shafts over the walls. The house was cold but Dad placed two wood burning stoves in the house to keep us warm along with the butane stoves. Our first winter there was exciting. We had not had this many rooms before and an indoor bathroom was really a treat. Prior to this we had only used outdoor toilets. We still did not have running water, but used pump water for cooking and bathing. It would not be long before Dad finished the inside plumbing and we had running hot water for baths. What a luxury. I remember one of our cousins coming to the house and sitting on our inside commode and saying, "wow, this is really modern." The majority of our neighbors and family out in this rural area still had outdoor facilities. Dad was looked upon as a real pioneer in this area. Some time that year we also began helping Dad finish out the house. When we came home from school we were given the assignment of painting, scraping used bricks and pulling nails out of discarded wood. Our dad was a carpenter, so during the day he would be working on construction or remodeling contracts and whatever scrap wood, or other construction supplies they would throw away he was allowed to take for himself. Dad took full advantage of the salvage material, and it proved quite helpful and resourceful for him. I remember scrapping off mortar from old bricks and then Dad using the bricks to brick the front of the house and to build a flower bed. We would spend hours after school doing these types of chores. When we completed these responsibilities we went inside to do our homework, clean the house and cook.

In Daddy's Words:

"As I said, in 1964, we were able to move in our own home. It had not been completed. You see, as the saying goes, "the plumber's faucet leaks, the mechanic's car is not running good and the carpenter's house is never finished". We seem to always fix the other folks and put ours off. The way I had to build my home was from the pocket as you get it and part time. I could not borrow money to totally build the house without stopping. The system would not loan me the money. Not that my credit was bad. It was good. With God's help, keeping me healthy and giving me the knowledge and time, it was done. When we moved into our home, my children's ages were Ruthie (16), Wilma (11) Winnie (10), Barbara (8) , Theodore (7), and Jackie (4) Although the house was not finished, we were a happy bunch for the first time in a long time. We had an indoor bathroom in the house. It didn't take long to realize that with the number of girls, I didn't have enough bathrooms. Our house had four bedrooms. I had to start making plans for a second bath and the house was not even finished. The living room and one bedroom were yet to be completed. By the help of God and in time, all was done."

One thing about Dad, he had order. Period. There were no exceptions to his rules and order. He believed in everyone in the house pulling their weight. We were given assigned duties each week and we did not mumble or complain about it. Every night someone, usually the oldest girl, was designated to cook dinner. The rest of us had chores that included chopping wood, pumping water, gathering eggs and cleaning the house. I really hated the assignment of going to the hen house. It was a well known fact that snakes also like eggs. There were many times that I would reach into the nest to grab an egg and see eyes peering back at me. Dishwashing became one of my favorite household chores. After dinner, someone was assigned to wash the dishes, clean the kitchen and sweep the floor. Dad was accustomed to doing housework since he had been functioning in a caregiver mode since age twelve, so there was no pulling the wool over his eyes. He always inspected the kitchen when you were finished. It had to be to his satisfaction or he pulled you up out of bed to redo the kitchen. It was not a good feeling to hit the cold floor at eleven at night to redo the kitchen after you've been snuggling in a warm bed for an hour. Our life in the new home settled into a routine.

In Daddy's Words:

" By 1965, we had began to call this house home and not just a place to stay. Many of the children's school mates began to come and spend the night with us. All seemed to enjoy being at our new home. Many mornings I would have the chore to make the breakfast for them to get off to school. Again, that is where my mother's training had come in handy and it was not a hard task for me at all. One of the girls would make the evening meal and one would clean the house. The one boy at home at that time had a chore to do his own room and some of the outside things that needed to be done. But to my surprise, I learned many years later that he did not do what he was supposed to do. One of his sister would always do it for him."

We spent most of our summers working in the fields to earn money for school clothes and supplies. Dad made sure we understood early in life that we had to work. We were not given an allowance, but we were expected to work outside the home to have our own money. Each summer we worked with a local hauler who contracted for pulling weeds out of bean fields. The work was hard. We had to get up at five in the morning to catch the work truck to the local site. We usually worked from 6:30 a.m. until about 1 p.m. We earned about five dollars per day, and worked Monday through Friday. One day after getting my five dollars pay, I tucked the bill in my shirt pocket. Forgetting I had money in my front shirt pocket, I rode on the back of a pickup truck home. Apparently the bill flew out with the wind. When I got home, Dad asked me where my pay was for the day, I could not find it. So, he sent all of us back down the dusty road to look for that money. Dad did not let you off easy; He wanted you to know the value of hard- earned money. I learned that lesson the hard way. We never did find the money. As a result I learned to be careful with my money. As a matter of fact, from that incident, Dad instructed me to give my money to one of the older sisters until I got home. Every dollar counted in our family so we used the money very wisely. We would put our school clothes in the lay-a-way at the start of the field work season, and then get them out at the end of the summer. After my introduction to cotton picking I was introduced to pulling up cotton stalks later in the fall. Following the picking of the cotton, the local farmers would have the same cotton pickers pull up the stalks for the next spring's planting. This process was much easier than picking in that all you had to master was enough strength to pull the stalk up from its roots. The season for this was very short and lasted less than a month. When winter set in there really was no additional means to make extra money. Dad hunted in the fall and winter for food for our family. He always planted a large garden in the spring and summer for canning and preserving food for the winter. We also worked the garden in the evening after school and during the summer. Dad planted a number of vegetables, among them corn, cabbage, peppers, okra, tomatoes and several types of beans and peas. We would can or freeze the vegetables for the winter. Dad loved coming in from work and getting on the small tractor and working the ground. It seemed to bring him contentment and a sense of accomplishment. I remember him sharing the story of the ant that puts away and stores his food in the summer in preparation for the winter. Proverbs 6: 6-8 "Go to the ant, you sluggard; consider its ways and be wise! It has no commander, no overseer, or ruler, yet it stores its provisions in summer and gathers its food at harvest." Dad, hunted for coons, deer, duck, quail, rabbit, squirrel and frogs. We had no choice in the meat we ate, except when he became a Seventh Day Adventist. We were not allowed to eat any foods prohibited in the Leviticus code for dietary regiments. During duck season we made additional money by dressing ducks for the sports hunters who descended on our local town. Stuttgart, Arkansas was known as the "Rice and Duck Capital of The World." We had opportunity to meet a number of hunters coming from faraway places to hunt in the area. Dressing ducks was another life lesson for me. Dad hunted ducks for food. We discovered there were people who hunted ducks just for the sport. Growing up in an environment that looked upon God's creation according to purpose, we believed that hunting meat was for survival. Many of the hunters after bagging their quota for the day would donate the extra ducks to us. Our local community benefited economically during the duck hunting season. I had cousins who would cook during the season at various duck clubs in the area. Dad had designed an area in our back yard where we would dress the ducks. There was a large cauldron under a fire that contained boiling hot water, after removing all the inner organs we would put the duck in the water to make plucking the feathers easier. After all the feathers were removed we would hold the duck over the fire and singe any remaining hairs. Then once inside the house we washed the duck thoroughly and put it in freezer bags. This served as another means to make additional money during the winter months. The older girls in our family would do day work for some of the wealthy white families in our region. I remember my sister, Diane, going to work for Mrs. Louis Berg. She was the wife of a local farmer, and often needed assistance with her housework. To make some extra money my sister would work there two to three days after school. She would come home and share stories with us about their home, the types of foods they ate and an overall description of life in "a white person's home." We were always quite fascinated by these accounts. Many times Diane would prepare meals she had learned to cook at Mrs. Berg's house. Around 1965 a doctor and his family moved into our area. They were Fred & Freda Eldridge and their daughter Sara. They were from the northern part of Arkansas. He had opened up an optometrists practice in Stuttgart. They had purchased a large farm and an old farm house about ten miles from Stuttgart. They were actually about two miles down the road from our home. They named their farm and property "Sara's Acres," after their only child Sara. They hired our dad to remodel this old farm house. Dad was excited about this wonderful opportunity. I remember seeing him poring over blueprints and drawings at the kitchen table at night. Years later, Dad would share how overwhelmed he felt at times with this big contract. I'm not sure how long he worked on this project, but I remember that the family gave a large Halloween party and birthday party for their daughter, when the project was completed. Many people came to this party/open house from the area. I remember that the home was decorated with a lot of lights and Mrs.

Eldridge had games all over the house for the kids to play. There was dunking for apples and hiding go seek. They were quite proud of the work dad had done in remodeling the old farm house. It had been turned into an antebellum type home with elaborate furnishings. They had chandeliers, white wool carpet in their downstairs bathroom and other equally regal furnishings throughout. The house was a two story, four bedroom, and three bath mansion. It had a sunken floor in the den with a wood burning fire place. They spared no expense in furnishing this home, and many in the surrounding community came to gawk at the opulence that you could only see on television or in a magazine. The Eldridge's settled into the community easily. Mrs. Eldridge hired one of my older cousins to help her with the house cleaning and to babysit their daughter, Sara. She also hired another local woman in the community, Mrs. Ella Mitchell, to do her ironing. The Eldridges were very generous and often would give away clothes to the needier families in the community. Mrs. Eldridge was a socialite by nature. She loved hosting cocktail and dinner parties. She and her husband were members of the Stuttgart Country Club, an elite group of wealthy physicians, businessmen and farmers. The Eldridges soon became premier citizens in the local community and Mrs. Eldridge got involved in all the social clubs in town. Mrs. Eldridge had a very compassionate spirit. She gave more of herself than many of the other farmers' wives in the area. She was an angel of divine love and great grace that God sent to our community. I would not realize for many years the great impact she had on me and many others. Dad continued to do work for them off and on as they needed him to finish off other projects on their large farm home.

In Daddy's Words: " After my cotton was laid by in 1954, my brother, Freddie informed me that the man he worked for was planning to build a huge grainer for cleaning grain on the farm where he worked and that he needed some more help. The farm was about three and one half miles away from where we lived. I agreed to help for a while. At least until September when the cotton was ready to pick. Then I had planned to work in the cotton harvest, haul pickers and even pick cotton myself. But that was about two months away. So I started helping to build the grainer from the foundation. I had never worked with a real carpenter, starting a new building. The farmer's name was Ed Tarkington. He and his wife, Ruth, were very nice people. They had two children, a boy and a girl. The carpenter's name was Fred Lawson, a local man, who was very manner able and easy going. I did not know anything at all about building plans. All I did was what I was told to do and when the need came, shown what to do and how. I did not know how big it would be or how tall. After all the string lines were stretched for the footing, the dirt digging began with a hand shovel. Many people called this tool the gospel spoon. The ground was really hard and dry. Many evenings we would water the trenches so soften them up. Finally, the concrete pouring time came for the footing. For that chore, it took six men. The concrete was homemade with a cylinder gas mixer and I want you to know that five men would sweat a good deal with that mixer. After a couple of weeks we got the foundation in. Then we started the floor joists which were on a concrete pier six inches high from the ground. After that were the wall studs to the total height. Mr. Lawson, the carpenter was a little afraid of heights. So he depended on me a great deal. Of course, I didn't know that at the time. But this I do know, that shortly after we started the floor joist and wall studs, he started telling me that I should go into carpentry. But I would say, I don't think I can make it as a carpenter. But he would say, yes you could make a good carpenter. You handle the tools well and know how to take care of them and you are not afraid of heights. You are also quick to catch on. My pay at that time was six dollars a day; His pay was one dollar and fifty cent per hour and included lunch. Most farm work at that time was about six dollars a day also. I was only planning to work until the last week of August and then to the cotton fields I would go. The last week of August came and the news had spread and had already gotten to the boss. Mr. Ed Tarkington heard that I was leaving that week. The news got to him from some of the regular farm help who I had told my plans. That week when pay day came, Mr. Lawson asked me if I like that kind of work. I told him that I did but that the work was dangerous for the amount of money that I was getting and I thought my plan to pick cotton was a better deal, in that I could make ten to twelve dollars myself picking cotton, besides hauling pickers. He told me that the boss wanted me to stay and that he would pay me more money and he himself really wanted me to stay because I was a good helper. Shortly after, Mr. Ed came out with our pay for the week. He asked me about my plans. I told him. I also told him that I did like carpentry, but it was dangerous work at times and it didn't pay enough, but I had really enjoyed working with them. I just needed to make more money and my plans would allow me to do just that, make more money. Well, he said, you are right Arthur. But I don't have enough money right now to pay you more, but I tell you what I will do. I will pay you one dollar and fifty cents more per day from two weeks after you first started and I will continue that until the grainer is completed. But I can't pay you that until I get my crops out this fall. Now I know that one dollar and fifty cents more per day is not much, but from where the building stood at that time, there was four more months of work to be done, rain or shine. He and the carpenter needed my help. Mr. Ed was and is the kind of man you could trust. I took him on. It was a God guided deal. I worked on that building the rest of that year. The first of November, Mr. Lawson had to leave to go to another job. With much of the building to be finished, I was left alone to do the work. But I didn't regret it. Many times Mr. Ed would tell me what he wanted me to do and I didn't really understand how it was supposed to be done. I would have a problem trying to figure out how to do it and wouldn't get much done as a result. But Mr. Ed never complained. My problem was after he would tell me what he wanted done, he would leave and I would have to figure it out. Many times I would get upset and just sit there for about a half hour just thinking. Somewhere about the last of the year, we got the grainer work done. Everything Mr. Ed had agreed to do if I remained on the job, he did and even more. As for my cotton picking plans, well, my truck made a little money. Many of the area cotton farmers would use it to haul cotton to the gin and pay me for each load. Had I went with my cotton plans, there could have been many days of rain and no picking. Taking Mr. Ed on was a life time career move. Shortly after the grainer was built, Mr. Ed told me he wanted a side shed on the west side of the grainer for clean seed storage. He showed me what he wanted and how he wanted it built. So we kicked right into the side she work with no delay. The Lord was with me in guiding me to make the decision to except Mr. Ed's offer. I worked the most of the winter until the spring of 1955. I started getting the farm

31

ground ready to get the crops planted and worked on the crops plowing and chopping until it was laid by. I had a cousin living close by who worked at the rice mill most of the time. He also farmed a small amount of cotton. His foreman asked him to see if he could find someone that wanted to work for a while. So he asked me if I wanted to help. I accepted the job and worked most all the summer at Producers Rice Mill. After I was laid off, I got the crop out and then Mr. & Mrs. Tarkington employed me again to help with more repairs on their home Each year after 1955, I would work some part of the year at the rice mill until 1959. I would work four to six months. We would then be laid off. Our pay at the mill was one dollar per hour. That was not very much. But somehow we were able to get by. It seems that Mr. Tarkington always knew when I was laid off, because he would employ me at his farm to do repairs. Around 1957, he raised my wages on free will. I must say, I really did appreciate that. One day he had me building a white picket fence close to his house. His wife, Mrs. Ruth, opened a window and called out, "how are you doing Arthur?" My reply was, "oh, I am fine," She asked how I liked that kind of work and I said fine. I like carpentry work real well. She replied that Mr. Ed really do like your work. Boy that went a many miles with me. That just made my day. I kept trying to farm on a part time basis. In late 1955, I had moved to another small farm. I lost most of the cotton crop on that farm because of the pesticide 2.4D I gave the farm up in 1957. I didn't make enough money to pay off the small loan; it was time to throw in the towel. We continued to live on the farm but I did not do any farming. I worked part of that year helping farmers who grew rice and the other part of the year at the rice mill until November of 1958. I was laid off from work at the mill again. I told many of the guys at the mill that if they ever call me back to work at the rice mill, I was not coming back. Of course, the guys told me that I would. Less than a week after I was laid off, Mr. Ed hired me to repair one of his tenant houses. I started the first part of November 1958 and continued until January 1959. My mind was made up. I was tired of being laid off from the rice mill. I would go into carpentry work full-time. Since I had worked as a carpenter for Mr. Ed many times, I felt it was only right to let him know of my plans before the beginning of 1959. So Id did. I told him what my plans were and how much I would be charging per hour. I planned to use some of my pay to start buying tools to work with. I don't think I will ever forget his reply. He said, " well Arthur, I am glad and one thing you can count on is anything I can help you with I'll help you and any tool that I have you are welcome to use, and if I make good out of this year's crop, I'm going to build my daughter and son-in-law a house and I want you to help. It would be after July. My reply was " I really thank you for offering me the use of your tools, but I really do want to have my own and the reason I want you to know my price is because I will be charging everyone the same this year; if my price is okay with you, then everyone else will have to be satisfied because I have done more work for you than anyone else. All was okay with him. My backup plan was if I did not get any work, I would apply for unemployment insurance. I never got to draw a penny of unemployment insurance. After I got the tenant house repaired, other small jobs from other people kept me going until July of 1959. In mid July, Mr. Ed drove up to my door and said, "Well Arthur, I am ready to start my daughter's house in two days. Here is the blueprint. I didn't know potatoes from beans about a house plan. He told me that he had also employed Orbin Robinson to help me and asked if that was alright. My reply was " yes sir, that is really good." Mr. Robinson was the best carpenter I knew around these parts and I had never had the opportunity to work around him and I welcomed the idea. It would give me the opportunity to get to know him. I knew his helper really well. We got acquainted on the job about the middle of July 1959. He explained the house plans and how to get started with the footing, block laying, and string stretching, mainly the basics. I took to him a lot and I think he took to me. I was only two and one-half mile from the construction site and could easily go home for lunch, but we all packed a lunch. There would be much talk at our lunch breaks. He was getting to know my people and many other things about me. Shortly we got the footing poured with concrete, using that man working concrete mixer. Then came the time to set the blocks. After we got about one half of the blocks laid, Mr. Orbin got sick for a few days and didn't come to work. I finished setting the blocks. When he returned he was somewhat surprised and said that it was good. Well, we had worked about three or four weeks when one day during our lunch break, Orbin asked, "Holt how much are you getting an hour for your work?" . I replied that I was getting one dollar and twenty-five cents per hour. He replied, that he was getting *one dollar and fifty cents and you ought to be getting the same thing. H___, you are as good as I am. My reply to Orbin was that I had told them that I was going to charge one dollar and twenty –five cents per hour this year and I was not going to raise it. H---, you good enough, was his reply. I didn't think so. No one can tell me that all white people are no good, and this was a white man, and by the same token no one can tell me that all blacks are no good. There are good and bad on both sides. Now the house we were building was an all electric home. It was known as the gold medallion home. The first in our area. It was supervised by Riceland Electric Cooperative for the wiring. Most of the appliances were supplied by Sears Roebuck and Co. We finished the house around November 1959. The supplies wanted to have an open house to show their expertise. We as the builders were asked to come to the open house party. Mr. Orbin came and also his helper with his wife. I also went but my wife declined because of sickness. One thing I must say is that those people gave me more praise than I felt that I rightly earned. We left that job and went to Mr. Ed house to remodel it. We were there about two months. We built new cabinets in the kitchen and installed new appliances. It was a complete kitchen remodeling. It was the first time seeing a walk–hung refrigerator. It was a total built in kitchen. It was also my first time ever helping build kitchen cabinets. These cabinets had fifty doors and twenty drawers. Mr. Orbin gave me the chore of building and installing the drawers. They turned out good. After we had started the project, Mr. Robinson could not get me to raise my wages, so he came down to the same amount that I was getting. That was encouraging to me. It made me feel like I was pretty good with my work. At Christmas time, 1959, Mr. Ed gave Mr. Robinson and myself a huge hog for the holiday. Mrs. Ruth found out that I liked chocolate cake and she baked one for me and my family. She continued to bake that chocolate cake for the next thirty years at Christmas time. In fact, my family began to look forward to that special cake. As I look back to those times, I remember those early years of working for the Tarkington's. Many people were led to hire me to do work for them because of the Tarkington family. If I needed community signatures of carpentry approval, I would put their names at the top of my referral list. In 1960, a friend of the Tarkington's came to me to ask if I had enough work for that year. He wanted to know if I would help Mr. Robinson remodel his home. Mr.*

Robinson and I took the job, but Orbin said to me, " Holt now we will start this job Monday morning and one thing is for sure you are going to get just as much per hour as I do or we both will walk off." The pay was one dollar and fifty cents per hour. We didn't have to walk off the job, we worked about two and one half months on the project. From time to time we did many jobs together, yes we had some misunderstandings but they were never racial. They usually involved the matter of my wanting to purchase tools for our work. I wanted to buy some along the way, but he vowed not to buy any himself. I was paving my way to go sole. I learned later that many people wanted me to go that way.

VISITING PASTOR
AND CAMP MEETINGS

Our father was an Elder in the Seventh Day Adventist church. Every summer he would host a weeklong camp meeting on our home grounds. Dad built an outdoor pavilion building to hold the camp meeting services. It consisted of an A- frame building with a wooden platform in the front that served as the pulpit area. He built pews and other needed tables for the meeting room. The floor was not finished so rather than have a dirt floor Dad poured rice hulls on the ground. Every summer the District Elder and other church members would come for a week- long revival. We had strict instructions we were expected to attend the nightly services. Dad would always prepare weeks ahead of schedule, making sure there was enough food, and that sleeping quarters were suitable. He also liked to fix a good meal or two for the group while they were visiting. I remember him purchasing lamb, a delicacy for sure, to serve the church family. This was indeed a luxury or delicacy, since we only ate beef and chicken once or twice per week. We dreaded the coming of Pastor Bartholomew because we knew it meant outside nightly church services in the middle of summer where the mosquitoes reigned. Dad screened in the pavilion but it did not deter the mosquitoes from nesting in the cool of the day in the rice hulls and resurfacing in the evening when fresh meat arrived. We would sit in the back of the building, giggling and swatting mosquitoes. We buried a few hundred mosquitoes in the rice hulls. Pastor Bartholomew would preach out of his soul each night and sing as well. Dad usually accompanied him on the guitar. We learned to sing a lot of hymns during these meetings. One evening Pastor Bartholomew was preaching and got so caught up in what he was saying he almost fell off the pulpit. We laughed and Dad just gave us the eye. It may have seemed as though we were disrespectful and maybe even uninterested, but I know now that even in those services God was doing a work on the inside of each of us. I know that many of the principles Dad used to teach us were based on the Bible and the teachings of Jesus. Dad disciplined us when needed, but he used the Word of God to bring us in line. We had a reverence for the things of God and a great respect for the church. But still, as children we were from time to time silly and mischievous.

Mandatory Integration
of Public Schools

In 1965-1966 the school systems in Arkansas were mandated by federal law to integrate. My oldest sister, Ruthie, was given a choice by dad to either complete the remainder of her senior year at the all- black school, Immanuel or transfer to the white school in Dewitt, Arkansas. She made the decision to go to the white school at the beginning of her last semester in high school. Dad let her know that this would not be an easy transition, as there were many who did not want the black kids to go to the same schools as white students. In January of 1966 Ruthie started at the all- white school in Dewitt. She was the only student from the surrounding community to attend. In September of 1965 many in the community went on to Stuttgart to integrate. Ruthie was the only one from our area to make the decision to go to Dewitt. She came home from school with scary stories about students and teachers calling her "nigger." She would relate the stories of all the challenges she faced each day.   We lived in a community of farmers and sharecroppers who had mutual respect for one another. Hearing these stories was very disturbing.   After arriving on the school campus the black kids as well as the whites stayed in their respective places. The teachers were very prejudiced and did not offer much assistance in learning. Ruthie said she was basically on her own with finding the answers to her questions.   Dad was a man who had faced many challenges in his life, so he would just reiterate to Ruthie the importance of standing and being able to withstand the challenges. He would say, life is about challenges and you have to not give in. Our education was important, and he wanted us to get a good education. Dad would take Ruthie to the bus line and see that she got on the bus without incident. But he made it clear that any struggles or challenges she faced at school each day had to be faced with courage. Ruthie knew she could not drop out but had to finish the year. She came home with an "F "in Literature but managed to get it together before graduation. In the class of 1966 there were between two hundred fifty and three hundred students and my sister graduated in the top one hundred, which was a testament to her perseverance and determination. Ruthie managed to finish her last year in high school with great difficulty. The following fall she would be attending college, something no one in our immediate family had ever done. Ruthie represented a barrier breaker for our family and her example of courage would help fuel and strengthen the rest of us. She seemed courageous and calm about all of this though and didn't seem to miss a beat. During that summer we were told that we, too, would have to go to school in Dewitt and that all schools would be integrated nationwide. Dad went to many meetings with other black parents to hear about the different things that would be needed to get their children ready for integration. Those things included current immunizations records, a health physical and additional school supplies. That summer we had to work especially hard to earn more money for school supplies and other items we needed. Up to this time we had been attending Immanuel School which was an all -black school in our area. I remember starting kindergarten or first grade there. On the first day of school my sister, Diane, walked me to class. When she got ready to leave I started crying. The teacher tried to console me but I was so scared. I must have finally overcome my fear because the rest of that day was a blur. In the fall of 1966 we began attending the white school in Dewitt. We had to walk about a mile or so to the end of our lane to catch the bus. The older white bus driver told us we had to go to the back of the bus. I remember Diane defiantly refusing to go to the back and forbidding any of us younger siblings from going there as well. The bus driver became quite angry and slammed the door closed. We took our seats in the middle section of the bus. As the other children along the route boarded the bus they sat as far away from us as possible. You could tell they felt as though we were contaminated or dirty. Finally, as the bus became more crowded, the students elected to stand rather than sit down next to us. When we made it to our schools, Theodore and I got off at the elementary school and Winnie and Diane went on to the high school. That first year was a great challenge as we confronted racism and hatred from the students and teachers. I wanted to go back to the all -black school, where I felt loved and welcomed. I was also having difficulty understanding the subject matters I was studying. I remember being in the fifth grade and working on math problems. The teacher asked me to come to the front of the class to work out a problem on the board. I had no clue and didn't understand the concept we were working on. I scribbled something incorrect on the board and the entire class erupted in laughter. I was so embarrassed and ashamed. Returning to my desk I wanted to sink through the floor. The other students were whispering," she is so dumb, the stupid nigger." I started crying and laid my head on the desk. I don't remember much more about that incident. I made a promise to myself that day that I was not going to be the dumbest student in any class. Years later I was in high school with some of those same students who were laughing at me that day. With the help of God, I became one of the top scholastic achievers in our class. We experienced many incidents on the school bus, as the driver continued to demand we sit at the back of the bus. One day he announced a new rule, that the students would be seated from the back to the front as they were picked up. Of course, we were the first students picked up so it automatically put us in the back. We didn't fight him on this anymore and resigned ourselves to the back seats, where we taunted and picked at the other students in revenge. That bus driver had a stroke the next year and we were assigned a younger driver who was also our biology teacher. He didn't seem as much a racist. But since we were the last students to exit the bus in the afternoon, he wanted to make us sweep and clean the bus before we got off. Once again, our defiant sister, Diane, walked past him as he was holding his broom. She told the rest of us to get off because we were not sweeping anybody's bus. That was the last time any bus driver tried to infringe upon our civil rights. We were young, but we were not stupid. We of course, would share these stories with Dad. He always backed us up, yet reminded us that we had to be obedient to our elders and not cause any trouble. He didn't punish us for refusing to do what the bus driver had asked. When Ruthie left in September for college it was a sad day for the rest of us. She had not only been our big sister but a surrogate mother as well. We did not want her to leave us. She promised to come home on weekends when she had the money for the bus ride. We missed her a lot, but Diane stepped up to the plate as our next surrogate mother. She was a taskmaster in many ways. She did not tolerate laziness in any form. When Dad left for work in the morning he would give the oldest child instructions for the afternoon chores. Diane was a stern, "take no prisoners" enforcer. When we got off the school bus in the afternoon, we had to immediately start our chores. Cooking, cleaning, washing and also getting our homework finished. We had a pretty good system in place that worked well for us. We worked in unity, and we knew if one thing was incomplete on Dad's instruction list we would all get in trouble. We learned to help each other out and get things done quickly. Our other incentive for completing our afternoon chores was getting to go outside and play basketball. We knew that we could not be caught outside playing when Dad got home unless we had completed all our chores.

Sister surrogates, Revivals and the Holy Ghost

Diane was a natural teacher and leader. She came home and taught us all that she learned at school or in the homes of wealthy whites. When she was taking French classes, she came home and spoke French to us and taught us a few phrases. She was quite the homemaker as well. Diane took a home economics class and would implement what she had learned in our home. For example, when she began sewing, she would make clothes for us. This was very helpful to us and extended our wardrobe. Diane loved to cook and would try all types of recipes. She taught us how to set the table properly, and would not let us have dessert until we had eaten all our vegetables. She was excellent in planning out menus, and making sure we had all four food groups as well as different colors of food. Our home was spotless as we all cleaned and made sure we kept the house in order. When Diane was a senior in high school she took part in an exchange student program and took a trip to Wisconsin. She was there for a week and spent her week with a white host family. She came back from that trip with lots of stories. We would sit on the floor in her bedroom and listen intently. Diane was also a great influence on our spiritual life as well. She had gotten saved and joined the church early in her teenage years. And our sister, Winnie, quickly followed suit. They joined the choir and became very active in the church. They would spend a lot of time in prayer and fasting. I knew that there was something different about them, and began going to church with them more often. They talked a lot about the Holy Ghost and being saved. I had a lot of questions and they tried to give me some answers. During the summer months, the church would have weeklong revivals with traveling missionaries and evangelists. One summer as we worked in the bean fields, my sisters were sharing their knowledge of God with other teenage girls. One day they were talking to a group of girls from the Baptist church about the

Holy Ghost and speaking in tongues. The girls did not believe in the Holy Ghost or the speaking in tongues, and said that we will see if we see you in heaven. For some reason I spoke out about what the scriptures said about the Holy Ghost. The entire group of older girls stopped in their tracks, including my sisters and stared at me. I was shocked that those words had come out of my mouth. I had not realized until that moment how much being in the church and hearing the Word of God had impacted me. I was equally shocked that they had taken notice of me. I was the youngest girl in the group. What did I know about the Holy Ghost? It was from that moment on I began to realize there was something about speaking about the Holy Ghost that caused people to listen. We continued down the row of beans chopping away at the weeds and chatting on about trivial teenage stuff. Years later the Lord would remind me of this incident , as He began revealing to me the call on my life for the work of His ministry. That same summer, our church, Mount Calvary Church of God in Christ (COGIC) had an evangelist conducting a revival. She was a missionary and a powerful woman of God. My sisters had been attending her revivals for years and had come home with testimonies about the move of God during these revivals. They encouraged me to come and tarry for the Holy Ghost. I did not quite understand all they were saying but wanted what they had. Our aunts of course were there as well. During the revival services the evangelist would encourage you to say the name of Jesus over and over, and call out "yes Lord." I did everything they instructed me to do, but did not get the Holy Ghost that night. Feeling discouraged and thinking I would be tarrying for a while, I began to wonder if I was saved. Our pastor had instructed all of us to go on a seven -day fast, which meant no food for that time. My sisters were very supportive and encouraging during this time of fasting and praying. They made sure I had the necessary fluids and rest as we went into the fast period. That same week I finally received the Holy Ghost baptism with the evidence of speaking in other tongues. The remainder of that summer was different in many ways for me. When I returned to school that fall, most of my friends said I looked different. During those years as a teenager, I was surrounded by both young and old women who loved the Lord and served Him wholeheartedly. One of our cousins, Bettye Jeffery, served the Lord during this time as a missionary. She would come home from her job in Little Rock every evening and conduct the worship service. This was about a one hundred mile round trip drive. Her life was fully given to the Lord and she taught us to love the Lord. Bettye served as a spiritual mentor to us and continues today as a minister and evangelist for the Lord. She was the daughter of George and Dewbaby Jeffery, the surrogate parents of our father and his siblings. The Jeffery family was pivotal in the church at that time. All of the sisters were actively involved in ministry there. One of the older sisters, Demetrius, was the wife of the Pastor of the church. She would encourage the young ladies of the church to hold on to the Lord, no matter what we faced in life to remember it was God that was our anchor. It was during these years my faith increased and God poured His grace even more into me. I would not realize until years later how God was shaping me for ministry and mission work. I had many incidences over my teenage years where I experienced the chastening rod of God through my father's stern discipline. One fall Dad purchased a bicycle for the five remaining children at home. We would take turns riding down the lane leading up to the house and down the gravel road about a mile or so. Dad had given us instructions not to ride the bicycle when the weather turned cold. One fall afternoon after we had finished our chores someone suggested we l go ride the bike, even though it was cold and windy. I vaguely remember someone saying, "You know Dad doesn't want us riding the bike when it is cold." Another sibling said, "well we can quickly go ride before he gets home." So off we went. We took turns riding down the lane and back. Unfortunately, it worked out that I was the last one to get my turn. As I started down the lane, I saw Dad's truck coming down the road. I started pedaling as fast as I could but was not able to escape the inevitable. Dad pulled into the driveway just as I fell off the bike and headed to the house. He caught up with me quickly and took off his belt and whipped me good. My other siblings had ran into the house and did not even admit they had participated in the act of disobedience. I really was mad at them for several days. They continuously ridiculed and teased me about getting a whipping. It would be years later before I would enjoy riding a bike again. This incident reminds me of needing an intercessor. I needed someone to intercede on my behalf and no one did. Jesus Christ became our intercessor, we had all sinned and fallen short of the glory of God, but HE became the sacrifice for our disobedience. He took my punishment and now I am free from all guilt and condemnation. Some winter evenings Dad would roast peanuts in the oven for snacks for us. Other times he would pop popcorn and pour butter over the top. He seemed to enjoy giving us these little treats. He also made sure we started each school day with a hot breakfast. Dad was a very good cook having to learn early to care for his siblings when both of his parents died by the time he was twelve. He would make homemade biscuits each morning for us along with a hot breakfast cereal. We would wake up to the wonderful aroma of fresh baked bread. That was hard to pass up on the cold winter mornings. Dad was very concerned about us doing well in school. He may not have graduated from high school but he was determined his children would get a good education. It was a solemn rule that you never came home with a grade below a "C." Period. One semester my sister Winnie came home with a "D" in a history course. Dad put her on punishment. She was the resident authority on every Hollywood movie and actor out at the time. She was the trivial winner hands down when it came to guessing who played in which movies. She would stay up late at night until the TV signed off watching movies. After the bad grade she was grounded from TV. Needless to say she pulled her grade up the next semester. After that incident Winnie knew next to nothing about the Hollywood stars and movies. Dad encouraged us to study and do our homework together. We would gather around our kitchen table in the evening and help each other. Our teachers knew the reputation of the Holt children to excel in their studies. So by the time I made it to high school my older siblings had set the mark for high grades. In May of 1966 Ruthie graduated from Dewitt High School. She would go on to college at Pine Bluff where she graduated with a degree in Sociology. She was our example of staying steadfast and focused on your education and getting out of poverty. Our high school years were spent primarily at DeWitt and we all graduated with honors from high school and most of us attended college or trade school. Dad was very proud of what we were able to accomplish in getting a good solid education. He had sacrificed so much of his life and worked so hard that we might have a better opportunity.

NANCY AND MS. FLORA

As I stated earlier, I wanted to share more information about our stepmother, Nancy. She was very young when she married our father. Suddenly a mother of six children ages three to sixteen; she took on the task with enthusiasm and love. We did not make life easy for her as young children. We were mischievous, and criticized her cooking skills endlessly. Our aunt Totsie had lived with us for a year after mother's death, and spoiled us with her great cooking. Nancy on the other hand could not boil water without a mishap. We were brutal in telling her about her shortcomings. Nancy had grown up in the St. Louis area and had been very active in the Apostolic Christian Church. Her faith, prayers and constant memorizing of psalms were probably what kept her sane. She had moved to Arkansas to live with her Aunt Flora when she met our father. Nancy was quite gifted in writing poetry and had mastered the art of memorization. She would often say an entire psalm from the Bible from memory. King David of the Old Testament was one of her favorites and she would quote many of his psalms. She relied heavily on her faith in God and the word of God to live. Nancy was not a very good driver. As a matter of fact I am not sure she ever really mastered safe driving skills, but she would drive the family car from time to time. She had several minor accidents with one or two of us in the car, and dad got to where he would not allow her to drive. One day I was riding in the car with her and as she turned off the main highway onto the gravel road leading home, the door I was leaning against flew open and out I slid. Sliding on the gravel, I just picked myself up and limped back to the car. That evening when Dad arrived home, I heard him talking to Nancy about me falling out of the car. Apparently Ms. Ella, the neighbor on the corner, had seen the entire incident, flagged Dad down on his way home to see if I was ok. Needless to say after that incident, Nancy drove us less. Nancy had lived with her aunt, Ms. Flora, before marrying our father. Ms. Flora, was widowed, childless and an avid fisherman. There were two things near and dear to Ms. Flora's heart, Jesus and fishing, and in that order. She was a stout woman, who had worked as a maid for a wealthy Jewish family in St. Louis. She purchased some property in Arkansas and moved there around 1966. Ms. Flora would play a pivotal role in our spiritual lives as well. She would leave home at six or so in the morning heading to a creek, pond, riverbank or reservoir to fish. She would fish for ten or twelve hours per day. Sometimes Nancy would go with her, but eventually with having small children to care for, it wasn't always possible. One day I asked if I could go to the fishing pond with Ms. Flora. Nancy insisted that I not go to satisfy Aunt Flora, she would keep me out there all day. But I was curious and I really wanted to see what kept her outdoors that long. So Nancy relinquished and said I could go. She packed me a lunch and added extra water to Ms. Flora's supplies. She gave me instructions on what to wear and made sure I had on comfortable sturdy shoes. We left about eight in the morning and spent most of the day at the creek. Ms. Flora would stay on the fishing bank most of the day. She used a cane pole and would prop up three or four poles. After finding a good spot and setting up her poles we sat down on the ground and waited. While waiting by the water Ms. Flora would sing hymns and songs of praise to God. She delighted in just looking out over the water and blessing God for His creation. I spent many summer days on the creek banks with Ms. Flora. She shared stories about her life, how she got saved and her love for Jesus. There were a few times that I actually caught fish, and she would show me how to clean and prep the fish. It was a life lesson for me. Ms. Flora died at the age of eighty -four and I was asked by my family to deliver her eulogy. Speaking at her funeral I recounted that "the fisher lady" was indeed an example of a disciple of Jesus Christ, who understood the cost and sacrifice to be a "fisher of men". Fishermen are disciplined, determined and detailed. They are patient, long suffering, and willing to sacrifice of themselves in order to catch a fish. Jesus told his disciples, "I will make you fishers of men". Ms. Flora was an example of a disciple and a determined fisherman. Her example of love for God, love for others and love of fishing prepared me for a life of ministry.

MRS. ELDRIDGE

Mr. & Mrs. Eldridge remained pivotal in our lives. When my sister Diane got ready to get married, Mrs. Eldridge insisted on coming to our home and decorating the house with fresh flowers and providing some of her finest china and silver to serve the food. Mrs. Eldridge became somewhat of a surrogate mother to us and would brood over us like we were her own children. After my older sister married and moved to town to work, I started working more for Mrs. Eldridge and less in the fields. I was very happy about that since it was so hot and humid in the fields. And the Eldridge home had air conditioning. I adapted quite well to the change of environments. Mrs. Eldridge seemed to pour herself into me, and made me her little chameleon. She would spend hours going over how to clean her home and would talk to me as though I would have a home of this same caliber when I got older. She was a pivotal person in my life. I learned the customs and ways of "rich" folks from her. I was promoted from the cotton fields to the "big "house. I had escaped the hot humid cotton fields and stepped up to the "air -conditioned" environment. My days of toiling in the hot fields were over at last. Mrs. Eldridge was wealthy and she spent a great deal of money furnishing their southern mansion. Many days while cleaning her china or silver she would share insights about life with me. It seemed as though I was an extension of their family. Whenever they had social activities in town they would invite me to join with their family. Their daughter, Sara, was involved in ballet and music lessons and I would attend her recitals with them. I could have never imagined the opulence and luxury of their environment. My exposure to their home and lifestyle opened up my world to other possibilities for my life. Mrs. Eldridge taught me many things about caring for fine furnishings and preparing a home to receive guests. Little did I realize that not only was she pouring knowledge into me, God was also using her to pour HIS great compassion, love and grace for others as well. This would become evident in my life later as God sent me to the mission fields of Haiti. Mrs. Eldridge had strong opinions about life and didn't mind sharing them with you. She believed in getting a good education and would stress often the importance of a girl "marrying" well. Each day while cleaning her house she would tutor me in the grace, manners and etiquette of the elite society. She and her husband would host two or three cocktail parties and dinner parties each year. During these parties I was allowed to peek from the Dutch door opening in the kitchen. There was always extreme excitement in the air and preparation for these events beginning weeks in advance. The house had to be spotless from top to bottom. I enjoyed these festive times. Mrs. Eldridge always hired two or three of the staff members from the local country club to serve at these parties. I was only there to assist with the dishwashing and clean-up. Mrs. Eldridge took great pains to teach me the finer things in life, including cooking. Once for a dinner party she was preparing asparagus with hollandaise sauce. She wanted me to help her prepare the sauce. In her "Betty Crocker" style kitchen she lovingly took the time to show me how to cook the special sauce to perfection. Today, when I see a recipe which includes hollandaise sauce I think fondly of her. Our relationship was more than just employer and employee, and it was in these special teaching moments that I see she was also a surrogate mother. God's divine hand was again at work, lovingly, patiently and with great grace instructing me on the little things that would help me in later life. One summer, Mrs. Eldridge decided she wanted to catalog everything in her home and prepare a manual that could be referenced by any staff. We started in her kitchen and laundry area indexing every item. Every drawer or cabinet , what could be found in them and what type of cleaning care necessary to maintain the item. The list was extensive and exhaustive. She was very enthusiastic about the project. This was a time consuming project and required that I spend two or three days per week working on it. This gave me an opportunity to make extra money for the summer. I wondered if this was not her intent all along. The project seemed like a waste of time and didn't make sense to me, but it was in my favor to spend three days in an air-conditioned house during the summer. So I readily welcomed the challenge. The formal dining room had a butler's table, a buffet and a china cabinet. In each drawer were silver, china etc. My job was to list what was in the drawer, the numerical count and indicate how often to clean the item as well as how to clean the item. The chandelier in the dining room had to be cleaned with a special solution and it was done twice a year. This manual was to serve others who would come to clean whenever she was not available to give personal details. This was a fun project and it allowed me to spend a great deal of time with Mrs. Eldridge. Around the fall of the year, Mrs. Eldridge always helped with the harvest. She enjoyed being out in the fields and driving the tractors. She could drive a loaded grain truck into town as easily as she maneuvered their new Cadillac. When I got off the school bus in the afternoon I would make my way to her house. At times she would not be there but she'd leave a note of instructions on her kitchen table. She would do housework for the first four or five hours of the day, and then head to the fields after lunch. One evening while I was still there cleaning she came into the house somewhat later than usual. While driving me home later she shared a dream she had had the night before. She said the dream was quite disturbing. She told me she saw herself on the tractor in the field and something tragic happened. She could not remember the details but woke up quite frightened and sweating. The dream seemed so real to her that it scared her. I am not sure if she shared this with Doc and Sara, but I was scared when she told me. Several weeks later while out on the tractor there was an incident that scared her and the foreman. They were both shaken up by it. However, no one was injured. She said that was the same night she had the awful dream. Sometime later, as my school bus was passing by the Eldridge's home I noticed a lot of cars around the house and in the driveway. I thought it was strange because usually if she was having a dinner party she would let me know in advance so I could come and help serve. When I arrived home I tried calling on the phone to the Eldridge's home but got a busy signal. I tried for over fifteen minutes and could not get through. I didn't feel good about seeing all those cars at their home, so I called the next door neighbor, Mrs. Ella, to see if she knew what was going on. When Mrs. Ella answered the phone she sounded funny. I explained why I was calling saying the Eldridge's phone line was busy. Then Mrs. Ella said 'You haven't heard what happened have you?" I said, "no ma'am, I just got off the bus and saw all the cars at the Eldridges' house." Then she said, "Mrs. Eldridge was killed today!" Wow, what a shock to my ears. I couldn't believe what she was saying. She began telling me all the details and it sounded like she was far off in a tunnel. My mind and my heart were both racing, as tears begin falling down my face. I realized t hat it was true what she was saying. She said Mrs. Eldridge was out on the tractor with Doc and the foreman. As she was going over the top of a levee in the rice fields, she took her foot off the clutch and the tractor tipped backward and buried her in the mud. Oil from the tractor spilled out all around her. Doc and the foreman immediately came over to pull her out but the oil was so slippery and it was so muddy they had a great deal of trouble getting to her. By the time they got her from under the tractor she was dead. Doc put her body in the back of his pickup truck covered with a sheet and took her to town. When he arrived at the local emergency room they pronounced her dead. Of course I was beyond stunned at this news. I can't even remember hanging up the phone, but as soon as I did, it rang again. This time it was Sara, Mrs. Eldridge's daughter. She said, "Barb did you hear the terrible news about Mom? Wasn't that sad? Dad and I will come down to get you and bring you to the house to be with us." Sometime later Doc and Sara drove up and I walked out to their Cadillac in a state of shock. Crying and sobbing they hugged me and tried to console me. As I rode with them back to the house I was numb with pain and sadness. I arrived with a house full of people and flowers. The one thing that struck me right away is I could still smell her scent all over the house. It was hard walking upstairs to her bedroom with Doc and Sara to pick out clothes for her. Doc told me that I was as much a part of the family as he and Sara and they wanted me to choose something from her possessions to keep for myself. I walked into her double closet and chose a chiffon pink gown that was one of her favorites. Of course it had her smell in it as well. I spent the rest of the evening there with the family, crying and remembering, looking around the huge house wondering how we could go on without her. She was such a forceful and vibrant spirit in my life and the life of many others. Life seemed to stand still that day for me. More than the loss of my real mother, this pain was beyond any I had experienced. Mrs. Eldridge was like a mother to me and had been so involved in my life as I begin my teenage years. I found myself feeling lost and alone, as never before in my life. The morning of her funeral was a blur to me. I was accompanied there by my father and other siblings. The eulogy and the service were short. I couldn't understand all that was happening to me, but I felt an intense loss beyond what appeared in the natural. The days following her death I was numb and lost. I did not want to go to the Eldridge house alone but knew I would have to someday. Finally after about two weeks I went back to my job there as housekeeper. I was alone the first time in the house. I sensed her spirit very strongly there. It was hard for me to climb the stairs to go up and clean the upstairs rooms. I was so relieved when Doc and Sara arrived home. I never let them know I was afraid to be in the house alone. Mrs. Eldridge's death stunned me in a deep way. The loss of her voice, guidance and encouragement sent me into an emotional downward spiral. A major anchor had been removed from around my life. My family never knew the deep sorrow I experienced from her death. In many ways Mrs. Eldridge's death was far more painful than my own mother's death. I was only a child when my mother died and could not perceive of the emotional pain that goes with being separated from a loved one. Mrs. Eldridge was a spiritual mother to me. She fed me with love and a sense of what my destiny entailed. She looked at me and treated me not as I was in 1971but as the person I would become in the future. God wants us to look at others as He looks at them. Seeing them not as they are now but as God has purposed for them to become. The following summer I spent my last days in that house. I had encountered some things that would change my life forever. I found out I was pregnant in the fall of 1972, and didn't know where to turn or who to trust. I prayed as never before for something bad to happen to me so I would not have to face my father and the church with this great sin. I suddenly realized that I had made a terrible choice and the consequences were going to be difficult. The summer of 1973 I continued to work for Doc and made enough money to buy baby clothes. My family finally found out and after great sorrow and stress came to terms with the situation. My father's sister, Sista, again came to my rescue. She agreed to watch the baby for me while I finished my last year of high school. That was indeed a blessing, as I had no one else to help me out. When I had the baby in July my entire family was there to support and encourage me. They did not judge me or ridicule me but love me. Many of my sisters gave me money for the hospital and doctor bills. When Doc Eldridge found out from my father that I had a child, he and Sara came to the house to bring a beautiful blue outfit for the baby. That would be the last time I would see Doc alive. Four years later he died of liver cancer. Sara left for college and following college married and moved to Nashville Tennessee. The following fall I started school at another high school and graduated with honors in May of 1974. Following high school I married a young man I had met my senior year. We eventually had two children. We attended college together where I majored in nursing. While at college I worked full time and attended college full time as well as raise the children. During this period of my life I was not attending church and did not think about church much. Some four years later after graduating from college and starting my professional career. I began having a series of things happen to me that caused me to look to God and the church again. I don't really remember how it began, but I remember longing for something, realizing that deep within my spirit man something was missing. I started trying to satisfy this longing in many ways; through my career, through purchasing material things, even through my relationships with my husband and children. But eventually, I realized that nothing satisfied this deep need. For the first time in my life I realized that there was more to life than what I had been experiencing and that I was not being fulfilled inwardly. Here began my journey with God to find my true purpose in life. God created us all for His purpose, and when we receive His salvation our journey begins to find that purpose. We may try many things to bring fulfillment to our lives, but it will all be in vain. (Ecclesiastes 1: 1-18) Until we walk in our God -ordained purposes we have not begun living the abundant life. The abundant life that Jesus talked about in John 10:10 states, "I have come that they may have life, and that they may have it more abundantly." Yes, I was "living" prior to this revelation, but I only existed. The abundant life comes through an intimate relationship with the Lord Jesus Christ

HEARING THE VOICE OF GOD

At the age of sixteen I found myself pregnant and unwed. I experienced a tremendous amount of emotions ranging from fear, shame, guilt, loneliness and hopelessness. I wondered if my life would ever amount to anything. I felt as though I had disappointed many people including God, my family and myself. I wanted something very bad to happen to me to remove me from the nightmare and shame I felt I was living. The statistics were stacked against me, a teenager, poor, uneducated, and without a mother. There were times when it seemed as though my life was over. My future looked bleak, dim and actually dark. It was during this time that I got a visit one evening from "Dewbaby" our father's surrogate mother. She called me out to her car and began talking to me about my situation.   She told me that my mother had asked her to look after us before she died, and she had over the years been watching us as a mother hen from afar.   She told me to be strong and keep my head up during this situation, and to tell my father that I was pregnant. I started crying because I was terrified of telling my father this disappointing news.   But, she insisted this had to be done. So after drying up my face and receiving hugs and reassurance from her, I went into the house to tell dad.   It went as well as can be expected in a situation like this. I really was sorry for disappointing my family. I remember sitting in my bedroom one evening alone, feeling despondent, lost and utterly hopeless.   Visions of a life as a teenage single mother, on welfare danced in my thoughts. Suddenly, I sensed this inner voice, saying, "you will not always be in this state, don't let this mistake define or delay your dreams." From that moment forward , I was determined to be all that God had intended for me to be, so I worked extremely hard my senior year in high school and graduated with honors.   Although my personal choices created hardship for me and my family, I did not allow it to destroy what God had purposed for my life. My family rallied around me and my child, giving us the love and support we needed in order to move forward.   Yes, we all make mistakes, but it is in how we move beyond the mistake that makes the difference. No one would allow me to feel sorry for myself or indulge me with pity. Our father always told us to keep on living and trusting God. Mistakes happen, move on. Years later as I looked back on this time in my life I see it was a defining moment or a fork in the road. With an inner strength that I now know came from God I moved beyond this incident and began finishing my education. During my senior year in high school I worked after school for extra money. I also qualified for a welfare check for my son of forty dollars per month. I took that forty dollars and paid my aunt "Sista" for keeping my son. She was such a source of great encouragement and strength during this time. She loved my son and provided him with daily affection and unconditional love. After school, one of my other sisters would pick up my son from my aunt's house and keep him until I arrived home from work. I worked in the local Piggy Wiggly store three to four hours after school. My focus was on trying to get into college the next year. All my counselors told me that my grades were adequate enough to major in the science field. After college I began working as a nurse at the local hospital. My family continued to grow and I resumed spending time with my extended family. My aunt "Sista" had become ill over the years, and had developed a disease called scleroderma. She was seeing a specialist in Little Rock, but was not getting any better. I had a tremendous amount of gratitude to God for her and all she had done for me so I began assisting with her care. During the winter of 1986 she developed renal failure, and after extensive conversations with her about the disease and the treatment, she told me she did not want to go on dialysis. Her decision was based on the thought of being a burden to anyone traveling back and forth to dialysis centers. She made an unselfish decision to forgo dialysis. She died within seventy two hours of that decision. Her death affected me greatly, as she has been such a strong source of encouragement and love to me during a very difficult time in my life. I know that God used her to keep me focused and encouraged. In 1986 I had come to the realization that my marriage was in serious trouble. After spiritual counseling and two trial separations, I got a divorce in October of 1986. Now, I found myself facing another long road in life. I was divorced with three living on a single income. I did not know how I would meet all the financial needs of my family. I turned to God once again as never before. It would be years later I realized God had been with me all the time. The divorce was bitter, ugly and a soap opera script for sure. During this time I experienced depression and dramatic weight loss. I begin crying out to God for relief, direction and help. What I heard and what I sensed to do was move. I needed to go back to school to further educate myself so I would be in a position to care for my children and help them with college. Moving was a scary thought to me, as I had not been more than thirty miles from my family my entire life. But I sensed that if I did not move the result would be more frightening than the move itself. I had to trust God as never before and believe that this was HIS direction. So I began researching different schools and specialties I could transition into without much time or money. I came up with nurse anesthesia; it required a degree in nursing and one year of critical care experience. All of which I had. The nearest school was located in St. Louis, Missouri. I had an older great uncle who lived in the area. I began talking with him and his wife about staying with them for a short period of time until I got settled. I looked for employment in the area and found a hospital willing to train me to be a cardiovascular nurse. I begin making plans to move. This was a total shock to my family. But they supported me. My family loaned me money for the move and assisted me in making the move. I moved to St. Charles, MO. in September of 1987 with my three children. We lived with my uncle and aunt for one month. Later that same year I married, Chris Holloway, a man I had been dating for the past year and whom I had known since high school. He was a great source of encouragement and support to me as I began applying to anesthesia school. Once we got settled I started working on my application for nurse anesthesia school. Many of the nurses I worked with told me story after story of how difficult it would be to get into nurse anesthesia school. They told me it was often a two or three year waiting list and that it was virtually impossible to get in the first time applying. They also stated that it was prohibited for students to work during school, as the curriculum and clinical load were exhausting. I knew what God had spoken to my heart and I did not allow this information to deter or discourage me. I worked the night shift and during the day began seeking more information about the nurse anesthesia school. One day I made a call to the school to request an application and find out about enrollment dates. The secretary who answered the phone said to me, "you are lucky, we just had a cancellation in the interview process and you can get an interview with the committee if you get your application and all other documents to me by this Friday." I could not believe what I was hearing! I know that this was divine intervention. I quickly got all the necessary paper work together and went for my entrance interview. I was accepted to the program and things started moving very quickly for me. I graduated from the anesthesia program in August,1990, with honors, thanks to God. I started working at Missouri Baptist Hospital immediately after graduation. While working there, I met an anesthesiologist who had been traveling to Haiti for eighteen years providing anesthesia for an ophthalmology surgical team. He asked me if I would be interested in going to Haiti. I quickly responded that I was not interested. He would continue to ask me to accompany him on a mission trip for four more years. In the fall of 1994 God changed my mind, attitude and heart about missions. When asked to go, I readily said yes. Many people who had traveled to Haiti told me my life would never be the same. I must admit I heard it as a cliché and not as truth. But, God forever changed my life when I made that first trip to Haiti in January of 1995. God changed my perspective, my attitude, my heart and my walk with HIM. My husband, Chris, was not at all excited about me traveling to Haiti. He ,of course, had heard all the negative reports regarding the violence, civil unrest and dangerous conditions. But as the time for me to leave drew closer, God gave him peace with my decision. Traveling on this first trip with me were ten others from the St. Louis area. There were four doctors, three nurses, one nursing student, a pastor, and the spouse of one of the doctors. Arriving in West Palm Beach, Florida, we met the remainder of our team members including Dr. Van Dine and his wife, Judi. Dr. Van Dine would be doing the surgeries for the team;. He and his wife had been traveling to Haiti for over twelve years. This was more than a medical mission's trip for me, I sensed it was something I was born and purposed to do. There was no fear or doubt, just a settled feeling. When we arrived in Cap Haitian for the first time, I looked around at the airport and sensed I had stepped onto familiar land. When asked by Judi Van Dine my first impressions or thoughts, my response was "I feel like I just came home." I would not realize for some years how profound that statement really would become in my life. My first trip to Haiti, changed everything about me, what I thought about God, my life and my "plans." My life would change forever from this first mission trip. On the flight to Haiti, I sat and reflected about my life, and how it could be possible for a poor black girl from rural Arkansas, who picked cotton for survival, to be traveling to a foreign country on a medical mission's trip. But God knew. He knew even before I was born what He had purposed for my life. He knew that I would one day be making a mission's trip to Haiti. While I was yet a baby in my mother's womb He purposed my life. Jeremiah 1 verse 4 says, "The Lord gave me a message. He said. "I knew you before I formed you in your mother's womb. Before you were born I set you apart and appointed you as my spokesman to the world." Each of us has been set apart and appointed by God for a specific plan and purpose. Sadly, many never find that purpose in life. What has bought me untold joy and peace is the knowledge that God has revealed a portion of my purpose and I have been blessed to be able to walk into that purpose. There is nothing that can bring greater joy and satisfaction than stepping into purpose. That is God's desire for each of His children.

Haiti is a country that will affect you in some way or another. Either you will love it or you will never want to return. God has to call you to this land or you will never want to return. The devastation that you see all around can be overwhelming, if you have not been purposed for the work there. I fell in love with the people and the country from the very first moment I stepped on the ground. There was a deeper spiritual connection to the people and the land. Unlike anything else I had ever felt in my life, somehow I knew this was a divine call. I loved the people and the people loved me. I knew this was not possible without the working of the Holy Spirit. That first mission's trip would ultimately lead to fifteen more over the next thirteen years. Each trip I would experience a deepening of myself to the people and the land.

HISTORICAL BACKGROUND OF HAITI

Haiti is located in the Caribbean, on the western one-third of the island of Hispaniola. Originally inhabited by the Taino Amerindians, this small island ,roughly the size of the state of Maryland, has six million people. The native Taino Indians were virtually annihilated by Spanish settlers within twenty-five years after Columbus discovered the island in 1492. In the early 17th century, the French established a presence in Hispaniola. In 1697, Spain ceded to the French the western third of the island, which later became known as Haiti. Once the Taino Indians were annihilated, the settlers found a replacement in the slaves from Africa. Following a slave revolt in the early 18th century, Haiti became an independent republic. Today Haiti is continually plagued with political, economic and social problems. Haiti remains the poorest country in the Western Hemisphere. The average household income for a family is less than three hundred dollars per year. Eighty percent of the population lives below the poverty line and two thirds of the labor force does not have jobs. Malnutrition and disease are rampant. A large percentage of the population is infected with the HIV virus. Many in the country do not have safe drinking water or access to sanitary living conditions. There is much squalor and abject poverty. Death, disease, devastation and hopelessness are evident in the eyes of many you see on the streets and roads in Haiti. It was in this environment that God sent me to a small village called Pignon to assist in the delivery of health care. I would provide the anesthesia services to the medical/surgical group during the week we were there. I believed I was going to help them and to provide something they desperately needed. I thought I would be an instrument of God's love and great grace. It would not take long for me to be brought to the realization that I would be the recipient of God's grace. I would be given something I desperately needed; something that would satisfy the longing that I had not realized was ebbing within me. God would let me see my need was greater than any physical need I thought the Haitian people had.   God has a way of using others to show you what is lacking in you. While watching the daily activities of the people of Haiti and spending time with them ,I saw that their faith was not placed in tangible things. Their praise was not predicated on what they could visibly see, but in what God had promised in HIS word. They did not let what they saw or hear hinder what they knew about God. It was refreshing to my spirit and woke up something inside of me that had been lying dormant for years.

My second trip to Haiti in 1996 was a different experience. We had only eight people on our team that year; four women and four men.   This was a dramatic difference from my first year with twenty- three on the team.   There were no other members from St. Louis on the team. I traveled by myself to Florida to meet the rest of the team.   Judi and Ken Van Dine made every effort to make me feel welcome and involved. Our first night in Pignon was interrupted by a burglar. During the early hours of the morning a young Haitian man broke into our mission compound. Thankfully, Chris Eastlake, one of the other nurses, was aroused and saw him standing in our room. She yelled and he left quickly. The four women in our room got out of bed and began searching around the mission house for signs of entry and to see if it was safe. The four men were asleep in the next room.   After searching for ten minutes or so we decided to go back to bed. Judi however, stayed up and got her flashlight to look further. She looked around in the dining room she discovered he was still in the building and yelled for assistance.   We all got up and then went to wake up the men. By this time he had escaped through a window. After the men got up it was discovered that money was missing out of their room but nothing had been taken from the women's room. It was difficult to fall asleep after this incident. I lay in bed thinking that as soon as daybreak comes we are out of here. I decided that it was not safe, and our intent was not to come here to endanger our lives. The following morning, as we had prayer and breakfast, Dr. Van Dine informed us that the authorities and the mission committee would investigate the incident thoroughly and we would all have to give a statement. He also said the guard that was on duty during the night had been fired. The mission organization was placing safety bars on all the windows. I was waiting for him to say we would be leaving because of the incident. But instead, he and Judi gathered their clinic supplies and headed off for a day of work in the clinic. I was astonished, and secretly ashamed of my attitude and my lack of faith. That would be a defining moment for me in the missions' field. As I witnessed two examples of Christ's disciples' committed to the work He had called them to, and trusting in HIS sovereign grace and protection. The Van Dine's would continue over the years to demonstrate to me and others an unwavering, steadfastness in what God had called them to do in Haiti. The many evenings of prayer and bible study in the mission house would spark a desire in me to study God's word and ultimately lead me to attend seminary school. Dr. Van Dine in many ways served as a pastor to the many team members who accompanied him and his wife on missions' trips. He always acknowledged that it was God who put the "team" together. The relationship I had with the Van Dine's was God ordained. A middle aged white couple from rural Allegany County New York and a black lady from Arkansas; How would our paths ever cross, if not for the divine working of God in our lives? They served as spiritual mentors for me in Haiti and examples of God's missionaries. Trusting, obeying and relying on God for everything, they yet serve Him in Haiti.

Trusting God I continued to travel to Haiti, each time encountering different situations that would challenge my faith in Him. One year, after spending a week in Pignon, as we traveled down the central plateau mountain to Cap Haitian we discovered the river had risen. We would not be able to ford the river in our trucks as we had done coming to the village. We had only two choices before us in order to make it to Cap Haitian to catch our flight. We could try fording the river in our trucks or turn around and drive another three and half hours around the backside of the mountain to make it to Cap Haitian. It was decided as a group that we did not have enough time to go back the opposite way, so we made the decision to ford the river. I cannot swim and the water was very high in the river. I remember telling my driver that I could not swim. He instructed me to roll up the windows and pray. The first truck got stuck in the middle of the river; our truck was able to navigate through the murky water with the help of a Haitian man who walked in the water in front of us, virtually acting as a guide. We traveled down the mountain without brakes and with much prayer we made it to the airport in Cap Haitian in time. God proved Himself faithful, time and time again as I traveled in and out of Haiti. There were many occasions were miracles were demonstrated. In 2004, God directed my husband, Chris, to go to Haiti along with another nurse from our church, Sandra Young. 2003 had been a year of great turmoil and unrest in Haiti, as the people were revolting against the new government. In January of 2004, things began to really get unstable in the country. We were scheduled to leave in February. When we arrived in West Palm Beach, Dr. Van Dine had us read the latest state department update and travel advisory in Haiti. He wanted us to decide whether we would continue on or go back home. We all decided to go with the knowledge that the situation was very dangerous. We had a good week in Haiti, and heard a lot of stories about problems and unrest in other regions of the country. The satellite telephones were not working in the administration office and there were a few other logistical challenges but all in all it went as well as could be expected. On our last day in Pignon, Dr. Van Dine came into the town to inform us of that his son Neil had received an email from Missionary Flights International stating they were not going to fly into Haiti because the airport in Cap Haitian had been overtaken by the rebels. We had no way home! We made our way to the administration office, and as a group began to pray and seek God for direction. As I said the phones were not working on the compound so we had no way to phone for help. As we sat there praying and discussing our options, we asked the administrator to try calling Port Au Prince for us. The phones were working again miraculously. We were able to secure a flight on an independent carrier to Port Au Prince and from there to Miami. God provided a way out of no way. We were on the last flight out of Port Au Prince before they closed the airport. The country collapsed into chaos after we left and it would be three weeks later before any commercial flights would fly in or out of Haiti. I have many more testimonies about the faithfulness of God and His sovereign power as I served Him in Haiti. Looking back over my life, I can clearly see the Hand of God, directing, guiding, providing and sustaining. Had it not been for the Lord on my side where would I be?

Reflecting back on my life, motherless at age six and a mother at age sixteen; all the obstacles and struggles I faced, I realized I was not alone. God was with me all along. He provided angels seen and unseen to assist me. He placed surrogate mothers, spiritual mentors and pastors in my life to help shape me. Ultimately, He placed Himself, His Spirit within me that has been the guiding force and transforming power for me. All that I am and ever hope to be is because of what God has done in my life. Growing up in a farming region, we understood the principle of seed time and harvest time. Planting season would come and we would be out preparing the ground to receive the seeds. Then when seed planting time arrived, we had to go and dig in the ground to place the seed in its proper place, making sure that the ground was fertile and able to sustain the seed. During the growing season we would water the plant, till the soil around the plant, pulling out destructive weeds. Watching over this seed took patience and love. We waited in great expectation for the harvest time. Then by midsummer we would begin to see the fruit of this seed come forth, whether as beans, tomatoes, cotton or corn. Our spiritual lives are similar. God uses many vessels along the way to plant and water. Then ultimately He brings forth the harvest in our lives. The scripture in 1 Corinthians chapter three verse 6 the Apostle Paul states, "I planted, Apollo watered but God gave the increase." God used many vessels along the way to plant seeds of truth into my life. As I was growing up in this small community, there were many people who planted a word of truth into my spirit. They watered me with the unconditional love of God, watched lovingly from afar, protecting me, guiding me, and instructing me. They were from various walks of life, different social economic levels, different educational backgrounds, diverse racially, and from different denominations of faith. Each one of them was used by God to impart direction into my life. God orchestrated and ordained my life and lead me to the mission fields of Haiti. There is only One God, who is Father of all, watching lovingly over His children. Yes, it was HIS divine Spirit in operation in the lives of those I have mentioned and many more unmentioned that allowed God to bring me into His divine purpose. If you are wondering today whether your life has meaning and purpose, I can assure you it does. You may not realize that God is using you to develop others. I pray that you would allow God to reveal your destiny and purpose so you can live the abundant life.

MISSION FIELDS

Traveling on mission trips to Haiti for over fifteen years God developed me for evangelism in a great way. I now realize that we are all called to the mission fields. The fields are all around us in our everyday lives. Jesus' ministry was His everyday encounters with those He met out walking and talking. So today we as the church have to begin to see the fields that are ripe all around us. Working in the field of health care, I see many people every day on their journey searching for healing and wholeness. They desire healing in their mind, healing in their body and healing in their spirit. They may not realize that they are searching for spiritual healing. It is important that we allow the Spirit of God within us to minister to their true need. A question we should pose to those we encounter is the same one Jesus proposed to the man at the pool of Bethesda. This man had been sick for thirty-eight years. When Jesus saw him and knew how long he had been ill, he asked him, "Would you like to get well?" His response was "I can't Sir, for I have no one to help me into the pool when the water is stirred up. While I am trying to get there, someone else always gets in ahead of me." Jesus told him, "Stand up, pick up your sleeping mat, and walk!" John 5: 1-9. We know that the story continues with the man being completely healed. Likewise those of us who work in the health "field," can see that when we encounter people we should ask them the right question. Asking them the right question is assisting them with getting into the pool of healing. Often times we are hesitant to ask because this is an uncomfortable area. But as ministers of healing we have to see the true need. God initiates missions, the Holy Spirit empowers missions and the church fulfills missions. Missions occur daily right around us if we would just open our eyes. John 3:35 states, "Do you not say, "There are still four months and then comes the harvest"? Behold, I say to you, lift up your eyes and look at the fields, for they are already white for the harvest." Yes the fields are indeed white around us and we have to allow the Holy Spirit to use us to minister true

healing. God's eternal healing results in lives that are transformed resulting in living the abundant life. God began my training for missions in the cotton fields of Arkansas and continued with the many long roads of life, where lessons were learned. God further carried me to a land very similar to my childhood home, to develop me further for missions. Today, as I serve Him in the ministry of health, I submit myself to the Holy Spirit to use me in the everyday encounters in the corridors of the hospital, in the operating room and in the lives of friends and family He has surrounded me with. "The harvest is great, but the laborers are few, pray therefore the Lord of the harvest would send forth laborers into His harvest." Luke 10:2
To HIS Glory and Honor
Barbara Holt Holloway

Scriptures from New King James Version Bible

Lucille Keaton Holt my mother

Mrs. Freda Eldridge

Arthur D. Holt my father

My sister Jackie at age two and me (author) age 6